LION HOUSE
INTERNATIONAL
RECIPES

LION HOUSE INTERNATIONAL RECIPES

Compiled by Melba Davis

Photographs by Russell Winegar/Panorama
Food Styling by Susan Massey

Deseret Book Compnay
Salt Lake City, Utah

LIST OF CONTRIBUTORS

Diane Anderson

Alexsander Ayrapetov

Laurie Balls

Rachael Black

Missy Blackmore

Alice Bleak

Jeanne Brodevsen

Sonja Brown

Ainomaija Brunson

Lee Burdick

Elaine Dorrity

Melba Davis

Cherrie Dyer

Carol Facer

Chris Findley

Julie Gardner

Suzanne Rytting Garney

Charlene Higley

Phyllis Hogge

Brenda Hopkins

Ann Jensen

Gloria Rytting Jones

Karin Kelgren

Maria Inez Llanos

Eve Loerbs

Wes Long

Sirpa McConkie

Sharon McGregor

Gerd Nielsen

Ivoni Fakaton McPhie

Brenda Mena

Sue Monk

Paulina Ortiz

Peggy Page

Carol Prodnuk

Amalia Quienteros

Janell Roundy

Kathleen Tait Salter

Al Smith

Carma Varas

Kent Ware

Nadine Weiler

Orpha Wright

Library of Congress Cataloging-in-Publication Data

Davis, Melba.
    Lion house international recipes / compiled by Melba Davis.
        p.   cm.
    Includes index.
    ISBN 1-57345-245-9
    1. Cookery, International.   I. Lion House (Restaurant)
  II. Title.
    TX725.A1D324   1997
    641.59—dc21   97-8704
                                         CIP

Printed in the United States of America

10 9 8 7 6 5 4 3 2 1   18961

CONTENTS

APPETIZERS AND BEVERAGES

Barbecued Pork Strips
China

2 pounds (bone in) pork loin or butt
3 tablespoons soy sauce
2 tablespoons honey
2 tablespoons sugar
2 tablespoons orange juice (apple, white grape, or pineapple juice may be substituted)
1 teaspoon salt
½ teaspoon Oriental Five Spice Powder (recipe follows)
1 clove garlic, minced
1 teaspoon minced fresh gingerroot, or ½ teaspoon ground ginger
½ teaspoon red food coloring (optional)

Cut meat from bones and trim into 2-inch strips. Put meat strips in a medium bowl. In a small bowl, combine soy sauce, honey, sugar, juice, salt, Five Spice Powder, garlic, ginger, and (if desired) food coloring. Pour mixture over meat and stir to coat well. Cover and place in refrigerator to marinate 3 to 4 hours or overnight, turning occasionally if necessary.

When ready to cook meat, preheat oven to 325 degrees F. Place meat strips in a roasting pan; reserve marinade. Roast in pre-heated oven for 1½ hours, basting occasionally with reserved marinade. *Serves 8.*

Oriental Five Spice Powder

1 teaspoon cinnamon
1 teaspoon anise seeds, crushed
½ teaspoon fennel seeds, crushed
¼ teaspoon ground black pepper or crushed Szechuan pepper
⅛ teaspoon ground cloves

Mix together cinnamon, anise, fennel, pepper, and cloves. Store in tightly covered container. Use in Oriental cooking.

Cheese Triangles
Greece

8 ounces feta cheese, crumbled
8 ounces cottage cheese
2 eggs
1 package frozen filo dough sheets
¾ cup melted butter (approximately)

In a medium bowl, mix cheeses and eggs together. Set aside. Cut a piece (2½ to 3 inches wide) off the end of the roll of filo dough. Return the large piece of remaining dough to package and keep refrigerated until ready to use. Place the small roll in a bowl and cover with a damp cloth to keep it from drying out, taking care not to leave the cloth touching the dough. Separate strips out of the small roll of dough, 2 or 3 at a time, and lay them on a clean surface. Brush with melted butter. Place 1 teaspoon of cheese mixture on the end of each filo strip and fold dough over it diagonally. Continue folding strip like a flag. Place finished triangles on a buttered cookie sheet about 1 inch apart. Repeat with remaining dough and filling mixture. (May be made up to 2 weeks ahead of time and frozen at this point. Layer in shallow pan with plastic wrap on bottom and between layers. Cover tightly with wrap.) Bake at 350 degrees F. for 20 minutes. *Makes 60 appetizers.*

Water Chestnut Cheese Balls

China

1 cup grated cheddar cheese
2 tablespoons butter
½ cup flour
½ cup pimiento-stuffed green olives, chopped
Dash cayenne pepper
1 can (6 ounces) water chestnuts, drained and chopped
1 egg, beaten slightly

In a medium bowl, blend cheese and butter together. Work in flour, olives, and cayenne pepper. Add water chestnuts and egg and mix until thoroughly combined. (At this point, mixture can be covered and refrigerated, if desired, until ready to use.) Drop by teaspoonfuls onto greased cookie sheet. Bake at 400 degrees F. for 10 to 12 minutes or until golden in color. Serve immediately. *Makes about 3 dozen cheese balls.*

Chicken Wings

China

3 tablespoons butter or margarine
12 chicken wings
1 small onion, sliced
1 small can (10 ounces) pineapple chunks
Orange juice
¼ cup soy sauce
2 tablespoons brown sugar
1 tablespoon vinegar
1 teaspoon ginger
½ teaspoon salt
½ teaspoon mace
½ teaspoon hot pepper sauce
¼ teaspoon dry mustard
1½ tablespoons cornstarch
Cold water

Melt butter or margarine in a large frying pan; add chicken wings and onion slices. Fry over medium heat until wings are brown on both sides, about 10 minutes. Drain pineapple and set it aside, reserving the juice or syrup. Measure reserved pineapple liquid and add enough orange juice to make 1¼ cups. Pour into medium bowl and add soy sauce, brown sugar, vinegar, ginger, salt, mace, hot pepper sauce, and dry mustard. Combine well and pour over chicken in frying pan. Cover and simmer for about 30 minutes or until tender, basting wings with liquid once or twice. Remove wings to hot platter. In a small bowl, add enough cold water to cornstarch to make a smooth paste. Blend in some hot liquid from the frying pan; then return mixture to pan along with the pineapple chunks. Bring to a boil over medium-high heat, stirring constantly until mixture thickens. Pour over wings. *Makes 12 appetizers.*

Swedish Meatballs

Sweden

1 cup milk
½ cup bread crumbs
2 pounds lean ground beef
2 eggs, lightly beaten
¼ cup grated onion
3 tablespoons chopped fresh parsley
1 tablespoon salt
¼ teaspoon allspice
1 cup beef broth or bouillon

Pour milk in a large bowl, stir in crumbs, and let soak for a few minutes. Add meat, eggs, onion, parsley, salt, and allspice. Mix together and shape into 36 small balls. Put meatballs into a large frying pan and cook over medium heat until they are browned on all sides. Pour beef broth over meatballs and simmer, covered, for 15 minutes. *Makes 36 meatballs.*

Stuffed Mushrooms

Canada

18 medium-sized mushrooms
½ cup dry bread crumbs
¼ cup butter or margarine
¼ cup shredded Monterey Jack cheese
2 tablespoons milk
1 teaspoon soy sauce
¼ teaspoon garlic powder,
    or 1 clove garlic, minced

Remove stems from mushrooms, taking care not to break caps. Chop the stems very fine and combine them in a small saucepan with bread crumbs, butter or margarine, cheese, milk, soy sauce, and garlic. Cook over medium heat, stirring frequently, until butter is melted. Fill mushroom caps with mixture. Arrange on baking sheet and place 6 to 8 inches under broiler. Broil until golden brown. Serve hot. *Makes 18 appetizers.*

Minced Clam Spread

France

2 cans (6½ ounces each) minced clams
¾ cup bread crumbs
¾ cup cracker crumbs
½ cup margarine, melted
½ cup chopped fresh parsley
1 large onion, diced
1 teaspoon paprika
½ teaspoon salt
¼ teaspoon pepper
¾ cup light cream
Crackers

Preheat oven to 375 degrees F. Grease a 1½-quart casserole dish. Drain the liquid from one of the cans of clams. In a medium bowl, combine remaining can of clams with its liquid, drained clams, bread and cracker crumbs, melted margarine, parsley, onion, paprika, salt, and pepper. Turn mixture into greased casserole dish. Pour cream over the top. Bake in preheated oven for 25 minutes. Serve warm with crackers. *Serves 12.*

Orange Cream Stuffed Dates

Pacific Islands

1 package (3 ounces) light cream cheese
¼ cup powdered sugar
1 tablespoon finely grated orange peel
1 box (8 ounces) whole pitted dates

In a small bowl, beat together cream cheese, powdered sugar, and orange peel. Cut a slit in the center of each date and fill with the cream cheese mixture. Cover and refrigerate until ready to serve. *Makes about 2 dozen appetizers.*

Polynesian Meatballs

Pacific Islands

2 pounds lean ground beef
1 can (10 ounces) water chestnuts,
    finely chopped
3 tablespoons soy sauce
1 tablespoon brown sugar
1 teaspoon dried parsley flakes
½ teaspoon onion powder
½ teaspoon garlic powder,
    or 2 cloves garlic, minced
1 cup apricot jam
3 tablespoons cider vinegar
¼ teaspoon paprika

In a large bowl, combine ground beef, water chestnuts, soy sauce, brown sugar, parsley flakes, onion powder, and garlic powder. Mix well. Shape into 40 to 48 small balls. Place on a large jelly-roll pan or other baking sheet with sides and bake at 400 degrees F. for 15 minutes. Meanwhile, combine jam, vinegar, and paprika in a small bowl. Serve meatballs hot with apricot sauce for dipping. Meatballs may be made ahead of time and reheated at 400 degrees F. for 5 minutes or until hot. *Makes 40 to 48 appetizers.*

Yaki Mondu

Wrappers

3¼ cups flour
1 teaspoon salt
1 cup cold water

Filling

½ pound lean ground beef
1 clove garlic, minced
½ onion, chopped very fine
1 carrot, grated very fine
Salt and pepper to taste
1 teaspoon soy sauce
½ teaspoon sesame oil
Oil for deep-frying

To make wrappers: Stir flour and salt together in a medium bowl. Sprinkle water over flour and mix with fork. Knead until smooth. Let rest 20 minutes.

To make filling: In a small frying pan, cook ground beef with garlic until beef is browned and crumbled very fine. Cook onion and carrot in the microwave oven with a little water until tender, 1 to 2 minutes. Remove from microwave and add to meat mixture. Stir in salt and pepper, soy sauce, and sesame oil. Set aside.

Divide dough into small balls (about 1 teaspoon each). Roll out or smash each ball into a very thin circle. Put a small amount of meat in the center. Dampen edges with water and fold wrapper over; crimp edges together.

Heat oil for deep-frying to about 375 degrees F. Cook yaki mondu a few at a time until wrappers are brown. Serve with Vinegar Soy Sauce (recipe follows) for dipping. *Makes 40.*

Vinegar Soy Sauce (Ch'o kanjang)

¼ cup soy sauce
3 tablespoons vinegar
1 teaspoon sugar
1 teaspoon finely chopped green onion
1 teaspoon toasted sesame seeds

In a small bowl, combine soy sauce, vinegar, sugar, green onion, and sesame seeds, and stir until sugar is dissolved. Refrigerate until ready to use. Sauce may be stored, tightly covered, in refrigerator for up to 1 week. (Note: Some vinegars are stronger than others in flavor. Adjust according to your taste.) *Makes ½ cup.*

Samosas

1 tablespoon vegetable oil
1 medium onion, chopped
1 teaspoon ginger
1 teaspoon garlic powder
1 teaspoon curry powder
1 pound lean ground beef
1 fresh tomato, chopped (optional)
¾ cup cooked peas (fresh or frozen)
1 package egg-roll skins or wonton skins
Oil for deep-frying

Heat 1 tablespoon oil in a large frying pan; add onion and cook, stirring frequently, until browned. Add ginger, garlic powder, and curry powder. Cook and stir for about 2 minutes. Add ground beef and tomato and stir-fry until beef is crumbly and browned. Stir in peas and allow to cool. Cut egg-roll skins into 4 squares. (If using wonton skins, do not cut.) Put about 1 tablespoon or less mixture in center. Moisten edges with water. Fold over and press to seal. Heat oil for deep-frying to 375 degrees F. Cook samosas a few at a time until golden brown, turning once. To reheat, place on baking sheet in 350 degree F. oven for 10 to 15 minutes or until hot.

Note: Instead of deep-frying, you may bake samosas at 450 degrees F. for about 10 minutes. They don't get as bubbly brown in the oven as when deep-fried, but this is a lower-fat alternative. *Makes 24 to 36 appetizers.*

Filling

⅔ cup uncooked long-grain white rice
2¼ cups milk
1¼ cups water
1 tablespoon salt
1 egg

Crust

1½ cups flour
2½ cups rye flour
1 teaspoon salt
4 tablespoons melted butter
1⅓ cups water

Other ingredients

½ cup milk
2 tablespoons melted butter

3 hard-boiled eggs
½ cup butter or margarine, warmed to room temperature

To make filling: In a 3-quart saucepan, combine rice, milk, and water. Bring to a boil over high heat. Cover, reduce heat to low, and simmer until liquid is absorbed, about 50 minutes. Stir often to prevent scorching. Add salt. Let cool. Beat in the egg.

To make crust: Sift together flour, rye flour, and salt. Add the 4 tablespoons melted butter and water. Stir until moistened. Form dough into a ball. On a floured board, knead until smooth. Divide dough into 24 pieces. Shape into balls. To prevent drying, keep covered with plastic wrap.

To assemble pastries: Roll each dough portion into a 6-inch circle on a lightly floured board. Spoon 2 to 3 tablespoons rice filling onto center of each circle, spreading to within 1 inch of edges. Fold two opposite sides of dough onto the filling, forming an oval "football" shape. Crimp edges along the center opening. Place pastries on greased baking sheets and bake for 20 minutes at 400 degrees F.

Brush warm pastries with a mixture of the ½ cup milk and 2 tablespoons melted butter. Cover with foil and let stand until slightly softened, about 10 minutes. Serve warm. If made ahead, cool, cover, and chill up to 5 days. To reheat, place in single layer on baking sheets and heat in a 350 degree F. oven until hot, about 10 minutes. These pastries are traditionally served with Egg Butter (recipe follows). *Makes 24.*

Egg Butter

Finely chop the hard-boiled eggs. Mix with butter or margarine. If made ahead, cover and chill up to 5 days. Serve at room temperature.

Hot Chocolate

4 ounces milk chocolate, chopped in small
    pieces, or milk-chocolate chips
¼ cup water
4 cups milk

In a small, heavy saucepan, place chocolate pieces and water. Cover and place over very low heat just until chocolate melts, stirring occasionally. Remove from heat and beat until smooth. Place milk in a 1½-quart saucepan and heat just until it boils. Add ¾ cup of the hot milk to the chocolate mixture, stirring until well combined. Then stir in remaining milk. Pour into mugs. *Serves 4.*

Watermelon Punch

4 cups puréed watermelon
6 cups water
⅔ cup sugar (or more, to taste)

Mix watermelon, water, and sugar together in a large pitcher. Chill several hours or overnight in refrigerator. Serve ice cold. *Serves 10.*

Sangria (Fruit Punch)

4 cups grape juice
1 cup orange juice
¼ cup sugar
1 apple or peach, sliced thinly
½ orange, sliced
½ lemon, sliced
4 cups club soda
Ice

Combine grape juice, orange juice, and sugar in a large pitcher; stir until sugar is dissolved. Stir in apple or peach, orange, and lemon slices. Just before serving, add club soda. Put ice into 8 glasses and pour sangria over it. Spoon some fruit into each glass. *Serves 8.*

SALADS

Cucumber Salad
Germany

6 large cucumbers, peeled and grated
Cold water
2 teaspoons salt
2 or 3 green onions, chopped
1 cup sour cream
1 teaspoon fresh-squeezed lemon juice
Lettuce leaves

Place cucumbers in a large bowl and cover with cold water. Sprinkle salt over cucumbers and soak for ½ hour. Drain and squeeze out remaining moisture. Pat dry with paper towel. Place in medium bowl. Add green onions, sour cream, and lemon juice. Mix well and chill in refrigerator for 1 to 2 hours. Serve on lettuce leaves. *Serves 6.*

Greek Salad
Greece

Salad

½ head iceberg or romaine lettuce
2 small tomatoes, quartered, or 8 cherry
    tomatoes, cut in half
1 cucumber, peeled and sliced
½ green bell pepper, sliced
5 scallions, thinly sliced
6 ounces feta cheese, broken into chunks
    (about 1 cup)
16 black Greek olives

Dressing

2 tablespoons red wine vinegar
1 clove garlic, minced
½ teaspoon oregano
¼ teaspoon salt
⅛ teaspoon pepper
⅓ cup olive oil

To make salad: Wash and drain lettuce and tear into bite-size pieces. Place in a large salad bowl. Add tomatoes, cucumber, green pepper, scallions, cheese, and olives.

To make dressing: In a small bowl, whisk together vinegar, garlic, oregano, salt, and pepper. Gradually add the olive oil, whisking constantly, until thoroughly mixed.

To serve: Pour dressing over salad and toss. Serve on chilled salad plates. *Serves 4.*

Carrot Salad
Israel

2 cups grated carrots
½ to ⅔ cup fresh-squeezed orange juice
    (about 3 oranges)
6 tablespoons fresh-squeezed lemon juice
    (about 2 lemons)
½ cup water
¼ cup honey
2 sprigs fresh mint

Grate carrots into a large bowl. Strain orange and lemon juices through a sieve to remove seeds. Pour over the carrots. Add water and honey and stir to blend well. Cover bowl and refrigerate for at least 2 hours to blend flavors. Garnish with mint sprigs. *Serves 4.*

Fruit and Lettuce Salad *Argentina*

Salad

2 medium apples, cut into chunks
2 medium oranges, peeled and sectioned
Lettuce leaves
4 cups shredded lettuce
½ cup chopped celery
2 bananas, sliced
1 cup broken pecans
1 cup halved cherry tomatoes

Dressing

⅓ cup mayonnaise
¼ cup whipping cream
2 tablespoons prepared mustard
¼ teaspoon celery seed

In a medium bowl, toss together the apples and oranges. Cover and chill. Line a large serving bowl with lettuce leaves. Combine the shredded lettuce and celery and place in lettuce-lined bowl. Cover and chill.

When ready to serve, toss apples and oranges with sliced bananas. Arrange fruit over the shredded lettuce in the serving bowl. Sprinkle with pecans. Arrange cherry tomato halves around the edge and on top of salad.

To make dressing: In a small bowl, whisk together mayonnaise, cream, mustard, and celery seed. Pour over fruit mixture. While serving, toss gently to coat ingredients. *Serves 10.*

Tomatoes with Seafood Salad *Chile*

4 medium tomatoes
¼ cup mayonnaise
¼ cup sour cream
1 tablespoon lemon juice
½ teaspoon salt
¼ teaspoon pepper
½ pound shrimp or crabmeat
Lettuce leaves
1 avocado, peeled and sliced
4 sprigs fresh parsley or cilantro
16 to 20 black olives

Carefully cut a hole in the top of each tomato, scrape out the center, and set tomato aside, saving the pulp. In a small bowl, combine mayonnaise, sour cream, lemon juice, salt, pepper, and the tomato pulp. Mix well. Stir in shrimp or crab. Fill the tomatoes with the seafood mixture. Arrange lettuce leaves on individual plates, place filled tomatoes in center, and garnish with avocado slices, parsley or cilantro, and olives. *Serves 4.*

Old World Hot Potato Salad *Germany*

6 cups potatoes, cooked in skins
    and sliced while hot
1 scant cup chopped celery
½ cup chopped onion
¼ cup cooked, crumbled bacon
⅓ cup water
⅓ cup white vinegar
3 tablespoons sugar
2½ teaspoons salt
2 tablespoons finely chopped
    green bell pepper
Pepper to taste
Lettuce leaves

In a large bowl, mix hot potatoes, celery, onion, and bacon together. In a small bowl, combine water, vinegar, sugar, salt, green pepper, and pepper to taste. Blend well and toss with hot potato mixture. Allow to stand for 10 minutes, then spoon onto lettuce leaves to serve. *Serves 10.*

Mixed Vegetable Salad
Korea

1 tablespoon sesame seeds
1 medium cucumber, peeled
½ cup vinegar
3½ teaspoons salt, or to taste
1½ cups water
1½ cups bean sprouts
1 tablespoon sesame oil
1 medium carrot, shredded (optional)
1 green onion, finely chopped

Toast sesame seeds: Place seeds in a small frying pan over medium heat. Cook, stirring constantly, until lightly browned. Allow to cool; then pour toasted seeds into a bowl and crush with the back of a wooden spoon.

Cut cucumber in half lengthwise, scoop out seeds, and slice thinly. Combine vinegar and 3 teaspoons of the salt in a medium bowl. Add cucumber, mix well, and let sit for 15 minutes.

Meanwhile, place water in a large saucepan and bring to a boil over high heat. Add bean sprouts, reduce heat to medium, and cook 2 to 3 minutes or until tender-crisp. Drain sprouts in a colander and rinse well with cold water. Place well-drained sprouts in a large bowl.

Pour the cucumber mixture into the colander and gently squeeze out excess liquid with hands. Toss drained cucumbers with bean sprouts in bowl. Add sesame oil, carrot (if desired), green onion, toasted sesame seeds, and the remaining ½ teaspoon salt and mix well. Refrigerate 1 to 2 hours before serving. *Serves 4.*

Pictured on page 11

Tabbouleh Salad
Lebanon

Salad

2 cups chopped Roma tomatoes
1 small red onion, sliced in thin rings
2 ribs celery, sliced or chopped
1 cup shredded red cabbage
½ cup chopped fresh parsley
1 cup tabbouleh

Dressing

⅓ cup seasoned rice vinegar
2 tablespoons vegetable oil
1 teaspoon sugar
Pinch of salt

To make salad: In a large bowl, combine tomatoes, onion, celery, cabbage, parsley, and tabbouleh. (Note: Tabbouleh, a cracked-wheat product, can be found in the specialty section of many large grocery stores. If the package has a seasoning packet, do not use the packet in this recipe.) Cover and chill several hours in the refrigerator.

To make dressing: In a small bowl, whisk together vinegar, oil, sugar, and salt. Chill in the refrigerator.

To serve: Pour dressing over salad and toss lightly. *Serves 8.*

Island Fruit Salad
Pacific Islands

1 fresh pineapple
1 banana, sliced
1 orange, sectioned and cut in chunks
1 apple, cored and cut in chunks
1 cup seedless grapes
1 carton (8 ounces) vanilla yogurt
1 teaspoon finely grated lime peel
½ teaspoon ginger

Cut pineapple in half lengthwise through the crown. Leaving shells intact, use a knife to remove the fruit. Cut fruit in bite-size pieces. In a large bowl, combine pineapple, banana, orange, apple, and grapes. In a small bowl, whisk together yogurt, lime peel, and ginger. Pour over fruit and toss to mix. Spoon fruit into pineapple shells to serve. *Serves 6.*

Coleslaw

1 head cabbage, shredded or chopped
1 onion, chopped fine
1 green bell pepper, chopped fine (optional)
3 carrots, grated
½ cup cider vinegar
½ cup vegetable oil
1 teaspoon salt
1 cup sugar
Pepper to taste

In a large bowl, mix cabbage, onion, green pepper, and carrots. Set aside. In a small bowl, mix vinegar, oil, salt, sugar, and pepper. Stir well and pour over cabbage. Toss until vegetables are completely covered. Chill. This salad can be kept in the refrigerator for weeks and remain fresh. *Serves 12.*

New Orleans Shrimp Salad

United States—Creole

1 cup water
½ cup uncooked long-grain rice
½ green or red bell pepper, chopped
1 small onion, minced
1 cup cauliflower florets
6 pimiento-stuffed green olives, sliced
1 can (4¼ ounces) shrimp, drained
⅓ cup mayonnaise
Juice of half a lemon
Dash of hot pepper sauce
Salt and pepper to taste
Crisp salad greens

Bring water to a boil in a small saucepan; add rice. Cover, reduce heat to low, and simmer 20 to 25 minutes or until rice is tender and liquid is absorbed. In a serving bowl, toss together the bell pepper, onion, cauliflower, olives, shrimp, and cooked rice. In a small bowl, whisk together the mayonnaise, lemon juice, hot pepper sauce, salt, and pepper. Pour over vegetables in serving bowl and toss until mixed. Serve on crisp greens. *Serves 5.*

Three-Bean Salad

United States—Southwest

1 can (16 ounces) kidney beans,
    rinsed and drained
1 can (16 ounces) black beans,
    rinsed and drained
1 can (16 ounces) garbanzo beans,
    rinsed and drained
2 ribs celery, sliced
1 medium red onion, diced
1 medium tomato, diced
1 cup frozen corn, thawed
¾ cup chunky salsa
¼ cup vegetable oil
¼ cup lime juice
1½ teaspoons chili powder
1 teaspoon salt (optional)
½ teaspoon cumin

In a large salad bowl, combine beans, celery, onion, tomato, and corn. In a small bowl, combine salsa, oil, lime juice, chili powder, salt (if desired), and cumin; mix well. Pour over bean mixture and toss to coat. Cover and chill for at least 2 hours. *Serves 10.*

Tabbouleh Salad (page 9)

Galician Tuna Salad

1 can (6 ounces) chunk light tuna in water
2 or 3 medium potatoes, cooked,
    peeled, and diced
½ cup sliced, cooked beets
2 or 3 radishes, sliced
2½ tablespoons lemon juice
1½ teaspoons olive oil
Salt and pepper to taste

Drain tuna. In a large bowl, break tuna into chunks. Add potatoes, beets, and radishes. Toss gently. Whisk together the lemon juice, olive oil, salt, and pepper. Pour over salad. *Serves 4.*

Beet Salad

Salad

2 cups cooked, peeled, and diced potatoes
1 cup cooked, peeled, and diced carrots
1 cup peeled, diced green apples
1 small onion, minced
2 dill pickles, diced
Salt and white pepper to taste
2 cups cooked, peeled, and diced beets, fresh
    or canned (reserve 1 teaspoon juice for
    dressing)
Salad greens, torn into bite-sized
    pieces (optional)

Dressing

1 cup sour cream
1 teaspoon beet juice
¼ teaspoon salt
Dash sugar

To make salad: In a large serving bowl, combine potatoes, carrots, apples, onion, and pickles. Toss lightly, adding salt and white pepper to taste. Refrigerate to blend flavors.

To make dressing: Whisk together sour cream, beet juice, salt, and sugar. Refrigerate to blend flavors.

To serve: Just before serving, carefully add the beets to the vegetables in the bowl. (If the beets are added too long before serving, the salad will be a deep pink, while it should be tinted only mildly pink.) Pour dressing over and toss lightly, or serve in a bowl with salad greens with the dressing on the side. *Serves 12.*

Tomato and Cucumber Salad

3 medium tomatoes, sliced in ⅛-inch slices
2 medium cucumbers, peeled and sliced in
    ⅛-inch slices
½ small onion, chopped
1 can (16 ounces) garbanzo beans
¼ cup red wine vinegar
¼ cup vegetable oil
2 teaspoons sugar
½ teaspoon salt
½ teaspoon oregano, or ½ teaspoon
    dried parsley flakes
Pepper to taste

In a medium serving bowl, combine tomatoes, cucumbers, onion, and garbanzo beans. Whisk together vinegar, oil, sugar, salt, and oregano or parsley. Add pepper to taste. Pour over vegetables and toss to mix well. Let stand in refrigerator for 1 hour before serving. *Serves 10.*

Clockwise from top left: Carrot Bisque (page 16),
Gazpacho (page 20), Vegetable and Sausage Soup (page 16)

Pita Bread Salad (Fattoush) *Lebanon*

3 pita bread rounds
2 tablespoons olive oil
1 clove garlic, pressed
3 medium tomatoes, seeded and chopped
6 cups bite-size pieces romaine lettuce
1 small onion, chopped
1 cucumber, peeled and chopped
1 green bell pepper, chopped
3 green onions, chopped
½ cup chopped fresh parsley
½ cup chopped fresh mint
⅓ cup fresh-squeezed lemon juice
1 clove garlic, pressed
⅓ cup olive oil
Salt and pepper to taste

Preheat oven to 375 degrees F. Brush bread with 2 tablespoons oil. Rub with pressed garlic clove. Cut bread into 1½-inch squares and arrange on a large, heavy baking sheet. Bake, stirring occasionally, for 12 minutes or until golden brown. Remove baking sheet from oven and place on rack to cool.

In a large serving bowl, toss together the tomatoes, lettuce, onion, cucumber, bell pepper, green onions, parsley, mint, and cooled pita bread squares. In a small bowl, whisk lemon juice and garlic clove to blend. Gradually whisk in ⅓ cup oil. Pour over salad and toss to mix. Add salt and pepper to taste. *Serves 4.*

Holiday Fruit Salad *England*

2 eggs, well beaten
2 tablespoons white vinegar
¼ cup sugar
2 tablespoons butter
1 cup cream, whipped
2 cups seedless white grapes or
    maraschino cherries, halved, or
    1 cup *each* grapes and cherries
2 cups pineapple tidbits or chunks
2 oranges, peeled, sectioned, and cut in
    chunks
2 cups cut-up marshmallows

In a small double boiler, combine eggs, vinegar, and sugar; cook over hot water, stirring constantly, until thick and smooth. Add butter; cool. Stir in whipped cream. Add grapes and/or cherries, pineapple, oranges, and marshmallows. Pour into a mold. Refrigerate for 24 hours. *Serves 12.*

Chicken Salad *Indonesia*

¾ cup mayonnaise
2 to 3 tablespoons cider vinegar
2 tablespoons vegetable oil
2½ cups cooked, diced chicken
2 cups cooked rice
½ cup salted peanuts
½ cup raisins
1 cup chopped celery
1 cup mandarin orange sections, drained
1 cup canned pineapple tidbits in juice,
    drained (reserve some for garnish)
Lettuce leaves

In a large bowl, combine mayonnaise, vinegar, and oil. Stir in chicken, rice, peanuts, raisins, celery, oranges, and pineapple. Toss until all ingredients are well coated. Cover and refrigerate until thoroughly chilled, about 4 hours or overnight. Serve on lettuce leaves, garnished with pineapple tidbits. *Serves 8.*

Coleslaw Cardinal

France

3½ cups red grapes, halved and seeded
3½ cups finely shredded cabbage
⅓ cup frozen orange juice concentrate, thawed
⅓ cup water
2 tablespoons cornstarch
Prepared mustard to taste
½ teaspoon salt
1 egg, beaten
Dash of hot pepper sauce
2 tablespoons lemon juice
½ cup sour cream

Toss grapes and cabbage together; cover and chill. Combine orange juice and water in a small saucepan; blend in cornstarch, mustard, and salt, and cook, stirring constantly, over medium heat until mixture boils. Stir a small amount of hot mixture quickly into egg; return egg mixture to pan. Add hot pepper sauce. Cook over low heat, stirring constantly, until dressing thickens; remove from heat and blend in lemon juice. Allow to cool; cover and refrigerate until serving time. When ready to serve, blend sour cream into dressing; toss lightly with grapes and cabbage. *Serves 8.*

SOUPS

Pictured on page 12

Carrot Bisque
Finland

1 tablespoon butter or margarine
4 cups peeled, sliced carrots
1 cup diced onion
1 cup diced celery
1 cup diced parsnips (optional)
Hot water
2 cups half-and-half
½ teaspoon tarragon
Salt and white pepper to taste
Chopped fresh parsley

Melt butter or margarine in a large saucepan. Add carrots, onions, celery, and parsnips if desired; sauté the vegetables briefly over low heat. Then add enough water to barely cover the vegetables. Simmer until soft. Put in a blender and blend until very fine. Pour into large saucepan and add half-and-half, tarragon, and salt and white pepper to taste. Heat through; do not boil. Ladle into serving bowls, sprinkle with chopped parsley, and serve hot. *Serves 4.*

Pictured on page 12

Vegetable and Sausage Soup
Portugal

6 cups chicken broth
1 pound kielbasa sausage, diced
3 or 4 medium potatoes, peeled and diced
1 small can (6 ounces) kidney beans
1 can (14 ounces) diced tomatoes
½ head green cabbage, coarsely chopped
1 medium onion, chopped
1 large carrot, diced
½ green bell pepper, diced
3 cloves garlic, minced
Salt and pepper to taste

Combine chicken broth, sausage, potatoes, kidney beans, tomatoes, cabbage, onion, carrot, bell pepper, and garlic in a large pot. Bring to a boil, stirring occasionally. Reduce heat; simmer uncovered until thick, stirring occasionally, about 2 hours. Season with salt and pepper to taste. This soup is even better made a day ahead: let it cool and skim off all the fat before reheating. *Serves 6.*

Cock-a-Leekie Soup
Scotland

2½ to 3 pounds broiler-fryer
    chickens, cut up
4 cups water
½ cup chopped carrot
½ cup chopped celery
2 teaspoons salt
1 bay leaf
2 medium leeks, thinly sliced
1 small potato, peeled and diced
⅓ cup quick-cooking barley
2 cups light cream or milk
⅓ cup cut-up prunes (optional)

Rinse chicken pieces and place in a large saucepan with water, carrot, celery, salt, and bay leaf. Simmer about 25 minutes or until chicken is tender. Remove chicken pieces from broth. Skim off fat. When chicken is cool, skin and debone. Cut into bite-size pieces and return to broth. Add leeks, potato, and barley. Simmer for 15 to 20 minutes. Stir in cream or milk. Add prunes, if desired. Heat through and serve. *Serves 8.*

Black Bean Soup
Cuba

1 pound dry black beans
6 cups water
¼ pound salt pork
2 cloves garlic, finely minced
1 teaspoon cumin seeds
1 teaspoon oregano
½ teaspoon dry mustard
2 tablespoons peanut oil
2 cups finely chopped onions
1 green bell pepper, chopped
Juice of ½ lemon
6 slices lemon
1 hard-boiled egg, chopped (optional)

Place beans and water in a large saucepan and soak overnight. The next day, add salt pork and simmer, loosely covered, until beans are almost tender. In a small bowl, mash together the garlic, cumin, oregano, and dry mustard with the back of a wooden spoon. Heat the oil in a medium frying pan; add the onions and bell pepper and sauté until tender. Stir in the garlic mixture, lemon juice, and ½ cup of the liquid from the beans. Cover and simmer 10 minutes to blend flavors. Add this mixture to beans, cover loosely, and simmer until beans are tender, about 1 hour.

Dip out two cups of the beans with liquid and blend in blender until liquefied. Stir liquid back into beans in saucepan. Ladle soup into serving bowls and garnish with lemon slices and chopped egg, if desired. *Serves 6.*

Pepper Pot
Norway

5 slices bacon, cut into small pieces
1 onion, thinly sliced
1½ pounds boneless lamb stew meat
Salt
Flour
¾ cup water
4 teaspoons whole black peppercorns
1 large head cabbage
4 tomatoes, peeled and cut into wedges
1 teaspoon salt
Hot boiled potatoes with melted butter and chopped parsley (optional)

Sauté bacon and onions until bacon is almost crisp and onions are tender. Remove to a large kettle, reserving drippings in frying pan. Sprinkle lamb pieces with salt and dust with flour. Put lamb into the frying pan with the reserved drippings and brown quickly on all sides. Add the lamb, water, and peppercorns to the kettle. Cover and simmer 1 hour or until the lamb is tender. Remove lamb from kettle. Cut cabbage into 4 wedges and remove the core. Cut each wedge in half crosswise and break the leaves apart. Arrange cabbage leaves, lamb, and tomato wedges in layers in the kettle, sprinkling cabbage and tomato layers with salt. Begin and end with cabbage. Cover pan and cook gently 30 minutes more or until cabbage is tender. This dish is traditionally served with hot boiled potatoes. *Serves 6.*

Fish Chowder
Canada

2 large potatoes, cubed
1 carrot, diced
2 cups water
1 teaspoon salt
Freshly ground black pepper
1 pound haddock or cod
1 medium onion, chopped
1 cup water
¼ teaspoon salt
2 cups milk
1 tablespoon butter

In a large saucepan, combine potatoes, carrot, 2 cups water, 1 teaspoon salt, and a grind or two of pepper. Bring to a boil; reduce heat and simmer gently for 20 minutes until vegetables are cooked.

While vegetables are cooking, wash the fish and cut it into pieces. Put fish in a separate saucepan with the onion, 1 cup water, and ¼ teaspoon salt. Cook gently for 20 minutes. Remove the bones, break the fish into bite-size pieces, and add the fish and fish stock to the cooked vegetables. Stir in the milk and heat through (do not boil). Top with a pat of butter and serve. *Serves 4.*

Mulligatawny

India

3½ pounds chicken pieces
6 cups water
1 teaspoon coriander
½ teaspoon turmeric
½ ounce fresh gingerroot, chopped fine
¼ teaspoon cayenne pepper
6 peppercorns, ground
1 teaspoon butter
1 onion, finely chopped
Salt and pepper to taste
5 cups hot cooked rice

Place the chicken pieces and water in a large saucepan, cover, and boil gently for 20 minutes. Skim off fat. Add coriander, turmeric, ginger, cayenne pepper, and peppercorns; cover and simmer until chicken is tender, about another 40 to 50 minutes. Strain broth through a fine sieve into a bowl; set aside. Remove chicken from bones and add to broth. Melt butter in a large frying pan; add onion and sauté until clear. Stir in broth and chicken. Season to taste with salt and pepper. Boil until thickened. Serve over cooked rice. *Serves 10.*

Borscht

Russia

4 large beets
6 cups water
3½ cups chicken or beef stock
Juice of 1 lemon
Sugar to taste
Salt to taste
½ cup chicken or beef stock
¼ cup cornstarch
1 cup sour cream
2 egg yolks
Sour cream
Chopped fresh parsley
2 hard-boiled eggs, diced

Scrub beets clean and place in a large saucepan with the water. Bring to a boil and boil until beets are tender. Setting beets aside for use at another time, drain 4 cups beet juice into another large saucepan and add the 3½ cups chicken or beef stock. Bring to a boil and stir in lemon juice, sugar, and salt. Combine ½ cup stock and cornstarch until smooth. Stir into soup. Cook and stir until thickened. Combine sour cream and egg yolks. Gradually stir 1 cup of hot liquid into egg mixture. Then, stirring constantly, slowly add warmed egg mixture to hot liquid. Heat through (do not boil). Strain. Serve hot or cold, garnished with sour cream, parsley, and diced eggs. *Serves 8.*

Pot on the Fire (Pot-au-Feu)

France

3 pounds lean beef brisket
¼ pound salt pork
1 whole onion, stuck with two whole cloves
3 leeks, cut in chunks, or 1 bunch green
    onions, sliced in 1-inch lengths
1 rib celery, cut in chunks
9 carrots, peeled and halved lengthwise
1 turnip, peeled and cut in chunks
1 teaspoon thyme
Parsley to taste
Water
1 tablespoon salt
1 whole chicken (legs and wings bound to
    body), 3½ to 4 pounds
6 potatoes, peeled
1 small head cabbage, cut in 6 pieces

Put beef, pork, onion, leeks or green onions, celery, 6 carrot halves, turnip, thyme, and parsley in a large, heavy pot. Cover with water and bring to a boil. Add salt. Reduce heat and simmer, covered, for 1½ hours. Add chicken, cover, and cook 30 minutes more. Add potatoes, remaining carrots, and cabbage; cover and cook 30 minutes or until vegetables are tender. Serve broth in soup dishes with meat and vegetables on plates on the side. *Serves 12.*

Sausage Soup with Csipetke Noodles *Hungary*

½ pound dried pinto beans
Water
2 tablespoons vegetable oil
1 small onion, chopped
½ pound smoked sausage
2 tablespoons flour
1½ teaspoons paprika
5 cups water
1 or 2 bay leaves
1 teaspoon salt
1 medium carrot, peeled and cut in thin,
    3-inch-long strips
1 small parsnip, peeled and cut in thin,
    3-inch-long strips
Csipetke Noodles (recipe follows)
1½ teaspoons white vinegar
½ cup sour cream

Place beans in a colander and rinse well under cold running water. Drain beans, place them in a medium bowl with enough water to cover them, and let soak overnight.

The next day, drain beans in a colander and set aside. In a large kettle, heat oil over medium heat; add onion and sausage and sauté until onion is transparent and sausage is browned. Add flour and cook, stirring constantly, until flour is light brown. Stir in beans, paprika, 5 cups water, bay leaves, salt, carrot, and parsnip. Cover and simmer over low to medium-low heat for about 2 hours. Bring soup to a boil, add Csipetke Noodles (recipe follows), and boil gently until noodles are tender. Reduce heat and continue simmering, if necessary, until beans are tender.

Just before serving, stir in vinegar. Place 1 cup hot soup in a small bowl, add sour cream, and stir until smooth. Add sour cream mixture to kettle and stir well until heated through. Do not boil. *Serves 6.*

Csipetke Noodles

½ cup flour
Pinch of salt
1 egg
1 teaspoon water (optional)

Combine flour, salt, and egg in a medium bowl. Knead until stiff dough forms. Add 1 teaspoon water, if necessary. Flatten the dough between your palms until it is about ⅛-inch thick. Pinch off ½-inch pieces of dough and drop into boiling soup.

Steak Soup (Ajiaco) *Chile*

1 large onion, thinly sliced
1 tablespoon vegetable oil
12 ounces top sirloin steak, cooked and cut
    into thin strips (leftover steak is fine)
3 cups beef broth
½ to 1 teaspoon salt
¼ teaspoon pepper
1 or 2 cloves garlic, minced
¼ teaspoon cumin
¼ teaspoon paprika
2 large potatoes, peeled and cut in strips
2 eggs, separated
½ cup cream
2 sprigs parsley, chopped

Sauté onion in oil in a large saucepan. Add the steak strips, beef broth, salt, pepper, garlic, cumin, and paprika. Simmer for 5 minutes. Add potatoes and simmer until potatoes are tender. Remove from heat. Beat egg whites slightly and add slowly to hot broth, stirring constantly. Blend egg yolks with cream and stir into soup, stirring slightly just to blend. Top with parsley and serve immediately. *Serves 4.*

Potato and Leek Soup
France

3 medium leeks
3 medium potatoes, peeled and sliced
⅛-inch thick
3 cans (10 ounces each) chicken broth
1¼ cups water
½ cup whipping cream (add up to ½ cup milk extra if you prefer a thinner soup)
2 tablespoons butter or margarine
2 teaspoons salt
¼ teaspoon pepper
Chopped chives

Wash the leeks by holding them by the root and vigorously moving them up and down in a sinkful of cold water. This will remove the grit from the roots. Change the water and repeat until the water is clear. Drain the leeks. When the leeks are drained, slice off the roots and slice ⅛-inch thick. Do not use the tough, dark green part.

In a large, heavy pot or saucepan, combine the leeks, potatoes, chicken broth, and water. Cover and bring to a boil over medium-high heat. Reduce heat and simmer 35 to 45 minutes or until vegetables are tender. Without draining off broth, mash vegetables in saucepan with a potato masher until they are fairly smooth. If they will not mash easily, soup has not cooked long enough. Let it simmer 10 to 15 minutes longer. Add cream and milk if desired, butter or margarine, salt, and pepper and heat soup just to the boiling point. (Do not boil.) Ladle into bowls and sprinkle each serving with chives. *Serves 5.*

Onion Soup
France

3½ tablespoons butter
6 medium onions, thinly sliced
1 tablespoon flour
8 cups beef stock
Salt and pepper
6 thin slices French bread
Grated Parmesan cheese

Preheat oven to 350 degrees F. Melt butter in a large saucepan; add onions and sauté until golden brown. Sprinkle with flour; continue cooking until flour browns. Add stock; season with salt and pepper. Simmer for 15 minutes. Toast bread in preheated oven until golden brown. Place in soup plates; cover with cheese. Pour hot soup over toast and cheese. Serve immediately. *Serves 8.*

Pictured on page 12

Gazpacho
Spain

2 cups tomato juice
1 cup peeled, chopped tomatoes
½ cup chopped green bell pepper
½ cup chopped celery
½ cup chopped cucumber
¼ cup chopped onion
1 clove garlic, minced
2 teaspoons snipped fresh parsley
1 teaspoon snipped fresh chives
2 to 3 tablespoons vinegar
2 tablespoons olive oil
1 teaspoon salt
1 teaspoon cumin
½ teaspoon Worcestershire sauce
¼ teaspoon pepper

In a large bowl, combine tomato juice, tomatoes, bell pepper, celery, cucumber, onion, garlic, parsley, chives, vinegar, oil, salt, cumin, Worcestershire sauce, and pepper. Cover and chill in refrigerator at least 4 hours or overnight. Serve cold. *Serves 8.*

Country Bacon Soup

Canada

1 tablespoon butter or margarine
½ cup chopped onions
5 slices bacon, fried, drained, and crumbled
1 can (10 ounces) cream of mushroom soup, undiluted
1 can (10 ounces) vegetarian vegetable soup, undiluted
1 can (10 ounces) bean with bacon soup, undiluted
1 cup corn (canned or frozen), drained
1¼ cups milk
¾ cup water
2 medium potatoes, cooked, peeled, and diced
Salt and pepper to taste

Melt butter or margarine in a large, heavy saucepan over medium heat; add onions and sauté until clear. Stir in bacon, soups, corn, milk, water, and potatoes. Season to taste with salt and pepper. Cook over medium heat, stirring frequently, until heated through. *Serves 6.*

Bouillabaisse

France

1 cup chopped onion
1 bulb fresh fennel, sliced ¼-inch thick and separated into rings
¼ cup yellow cornmeal
1 cup clam juice
2 cans (14 ounces each) chicken broth
1 can (28 ounces) Italian-style tomatoes
1 can (6 ounce) tomato paste
2 bay leaves
1 tablespoon basil
1 teaspoon finely chopped fresh garlic
½ teaspoon salt
½ teaspoon coarsely ground black pepper
2 tablespoons olive oil
2 tablespoons red wine vinegar
1 pound fresh or frozen raw shrimp
1 pound swordfish steaks, cut into 1½-inch pieces
1 pound red snapper fillets, skinned and cut into 1½-inch pieces
1 pound mussels in shell, scrubbed

In a large kettle, combine onion, fennel, cornmeal, clam juice, chicken broth, tomatoes, tomato paste, bay leaves, basil, garlic, salt, pepper, olive oil, and vinegar. Place over medium heat and cook, stirring occasionally, for 1 to 1½ hours or until slightly thickened. While broth is cooking, peel and devein shrimp, leaving tails intact. Set aside. (If shrimp is frozen, do not thaw; peel under cold running water.) Add swordfish, red snapper, and mussels in shells to broth mixture. Continue cooking, stirring occasionally, until seafood flakes with a fork and mussels open (10 to 15 minutes). Stir in shrimp and continue cooking until shrimp turn pink (4 to 6 minutes). Remove and discard bay leaves and any unopened mussels. Ladle into bowls. *Serves 8.*

Minestrone

1 can (16 ounces) kidney beans, drained
1 clove garlic, minced
½ teaspoon salt
¼ teaspoon pepper
1 tablespoon vegetable oil
¼ cup chopped fresh parsley
1 small, unpeeled zucchini, diced
2 ribs celery with leaves, finely chopped
2 small carrots, peeled and diced
1 small onion, minced
1 can (14½ ounces) diced tomatoes
3 tablespoons butter or margarine
2½ cups water
⅓ cup uncooked elbow macaroni
½ cup beef bouillon or tomato juice
Salt to taste

Mash beans slightly in the bottom of a large kettle. Stir in garlic, salt, pepper, oil, and parsley. Add zucchini, celery, carrots, onion, tomatoes, butter or margarine, and water. Bring to a boil over medium heat, stirring occasionally. Reduce heat, cover, and simmer 1 hour, stirring occasionally. Add macaroni and beef bouillon or tomato juice. Simmer 15 minutes or until macaroni is tender, stirring occasionally. Add salt to taste. *Serves 10.*

Gumbo

12 ounces Italian sausage links, cut into
   ½-inch pieces
1 can (28 ounces) tomatoes, quartered
4 skinless, boneless chicken breast halves,
   cut into quarters
3 cups water
1 can (14 ounces) chicken broth
1 medium onion, thinly sliced
½ cup uncooked long-grain rice
1 bay leaf
½ teaspoon thyme leaves
½ teaspoon finely chopped fresh garlic
¼ teaspoon coarsely ground pepper
⅛ teaspoon cayenne pepper
2 medium zucchini, sliced ¼-inch thick

Cook sausage over medium-high heat in a large kettle until browned (6 to 8 minutes). Drain off fat. Add tomatoes with liquid, chicken, water, chicken broth, onion, rice, bay leaf, thyme, garlic, pepper, and cayenne pepper. Continue cooking, stirring occasionally, until soup comes to a full boil. Reduce heat to medium and cook uncovered, stirring occasionally, until rice is tender and soup is slightly thickened (about 30 minutes). Add zucchini and cook an additional 4 to 6 minutes or until zucchini is tender-crisp. Discard bay leaf and ladle soup into bowls. *Serves 6.*

BREADS

Stollen
Germany

4½ cups flour
1 package active dry yeast
¼ teaspoon ground cardamom
1¼ cups milk
½ cup butter or margarine
¼ cup sugar
1 teaspoon salt
1 egg, slightly beaten
1 cup raisins
¼ cup chopped mixed candied fruits
¼ cup dried currants
¼ cup chopped blanched almonds
2 tablespoons finely shredded orange peel
1 tablespoon finely shredded lemon peel
1½ cups powdered sugar
1 to 2 tablespoons water
½ teaspoon vanilla

In a large mixing bowl, combine 2 cups of the flour, yeast, and cardamom. In a small saucepan, heat milk, butter or margarine, sugar, and salt, stirring constantly, until mixture is just warm (115–120 degrees F.) and butter is almost melted. Add to flour mixture along with slightly beaten egg. Beat at low speed 30 seconds, scraping bowl constantly. Increase speed to high and beat an additional 3 minutes. Work in as much of the remaining flour as you can stir in with a spoon. Add raisins, candied fruits, currants, almonds, and orange and lemon peel; stir well. Turn out onto a lightly floured surface and knead in enough of the remaining flour to make a soft dough. Continue kneading until smooth (5 to 8 minutes). Place dough in a greased bowl, turning once to grease top. Cover and let rise in a warm place until double (1½ to 2 hours).

Punch dough down and turn it out onto a lightly floured surface. Divide dough in thirds, cover, and let it rest 10 minutes. Roll one piece of dough into a rectangle about 10 x 6 inches. Without stretching, fold the long side over to within 1 inch of the opposite side; seal. Place on greased baking sheet. Repeat with remaining dough. Cover and let rise until almost double (about 1 hour). Bake at 375 degrees F. for 18 to 20 minutes.

In a medium bowl, mix powdered sugar, 1 tablespoon water, and vanilla until smooth. Stir in additional water if needed. Drizzle over warm loaves. *Makes 3 loaves.*

Dorset Scones
England

2 cups flour
3 tablespoons sugar
1 tablespoon baking powder
½ teaspoon salt
½ teaspoon nutmeg
½ cup butter, chilled and cut in small pieces
1 egg
½ cup milk (approximately)
⅓ cup dried currants

Preheat oven to 450 degrees F. In a large bowl, mix flour, sugar, baking powder, salt, and nutmeg. Cut in cold butter with a pastry blender until mixture looks like coarse meal. Whisk egg and divide it in half. Beat 1 tablespoon of the milk into half of the egg and set aside. Add enough milk to the remaining half to make ½ cup liquid. Mix with dry ingredients until just combined. Add currants. Turn dough out on floured board, roll it out ½-inch thick, and cut with biscuit cutter. Place scones on ungreased cookie sheet. Brush tops with the reserved egg-milk mixture. Bake at 450 degrees F. about 15 minutes. Serve with thick clotted cream or whipped cream and fruit preserves. *Serves 12.*

Cornmeal Rolls

United States—Amish

2 cups milk
½ cup melted vegetable shortening
½ cup sugar
⅓ cup cornmeal
1 teaspoon salt
1 package active dry yeast
¼ cup lukewarm water
2 eggs, beaten
4 cups flour
Melted butter

In a double boiler, combine milk, melted shortening, sugar, cornmeal, and salt. Cook, stirring frequently, until the mixture is thick. Cool to lukewarm. Dissolve yeast in ¼ cup lukewarm water. Add the yeast mixture and the eggs to the cornmeal mixture and beat well. Let rise in a greased bowl for 2 hours; then add the flour to form a soft dough. Knead lightly, then replace dough in the greased bowl, cover, and let rise for 1 hour. Knead the dough again. Roll out dough on a floured surface and cut it with a biscuit cutter. Brush the dough pieces with melted butter, then crease them and fold in half. Place on a greased cookie sheet. Let rise for 1 hour. Bake at 375 degrees F. for 15 minutes. *Makes 3 dozen rolls.*

Braided Bread (Zupfa)

Switzerland

1 cup butter or margarine
2 cups milk
1 cup warm water
¼ cup sugar
1 tablespoon salt
5 eggs
3 tablespoons active dry yeast
11 cups flour
1 egg
1 tablespoon water

In a medium saucepan, melt butter or margarine with milk. Do not boil. Allow to cool slightly. In a very large mixing bowl, combine milk mixture, warm water, sugar, salt, 5 eggs, yeast, and flour. Beat mixture until you have a soft dough. If mixing by hand, turn dough onto a lightly floured surface and knead for 7 minutes, or until dough is smooth and has a satin look. Place in a large greased bowl, cover, and let rise until double.

Punch dough down and divide it into 6 parts. Work with 1 part at a time. Divide portion of dough into 3 pieces. Roll each of the 3 pieces into a 12-inch rope. Pinch all 3 ropes together at one end and braid them together. Pinch the ends together again at the end to finish the loaf. Repeat with the rest of the dough until you have 6 loaves. Grease 2 large baking sheets and place 3 loaves on each sheet. Let rise until double. Brush tops with 1 egg beaten together with 1 tablespoon water. Bake at 350 degrees F. for 40 minutes. *Makes 6 small loaves.*

Oatmeal Casserole Bread

Canada

1 cup lukewarm water
2 teaspoons sugar
2 packages active dry yeast
1 cup boiling water
⅓ cup shortening
1 cup rolled oats
½ cup light molasses
1 tablespoon salt
2 eggs, beaten
5½ cups flour

Dissolve 2 teaspoons sugar in lukewarm water. Sprinkle yeast on top. Cover and let stand 10 minutes, then stir well. In a large mixer bowl, stir boiling water and shortening together until shortening is melted. Add oats, molasses, and salt. Blend well and cool to lukewarm. Stir in beaten eggs and yeast mixture. Fold in the flour and mix well. Place dough in greased mixing bowl, cover, and refrigerate for at least 2 hours. Turn chilled dough out on floured board and shape into 2 loaves. Place in 9 x 5-inch loaf pans, cover, and let rise until double (about 2 hours). Bake at 350 degrees F. for 1 hour. Remove from pans immediately and cool on a wire rack. *Makes 2 loaves.*

Tango Biscuits

1 cup raisins
1 cup hot water
1 cup sugar
1 teaspoon soda
2 eggs
1 cup melted margarine
2½ cups flour
1 cup chopped walnuts

Preheat oven to 350 degrees F. Soak the raisins in the hot water for 10 minutes. Drain and chop in a food processor or blender. In a medium mixer bowl, beat sugar, soda, and eggs together. Add melted margarine gradually to the sugar mixture and beat well. Add flour, raisins, and nuts. Blend well. Drop by teaspoonsful onto a greased cookie sheet. Bake to 10 to 12 minutes or until light brown. *Makes 3 dozen.*

Soda Bread

4 to 4½ cups flour
¼ cup sugar
1 tablespoon baking powder
1 teaspoon salt
1 teaspoon baking soda
⅛ teaspoon ground cardamom or coriander
4 tablespoons firm butter or margarine, cut into small pieces
1¾ cups buttermilk
1 egg
¼ cup raisins or currants (optional)

Preheat oven to 375 degrees F. Lightly grease two 8-inch round baking pans. Set aside. In a large bowl, place 4 cups of the flour, sugar, baking powder, salt, baking soda, and cardamom or coriander. Mix well. Using a pastry blender, cut butter or margarine into the flour mixture. Beat together buttermilk and egg in a small bowl; pour all at once into flour mixture and stir just until dry ingredients are moistened. Stir in raisins or currants, if desired. Turn out onto a floured board and knead gently until smooth (2 to 3 minutes). Divide dough in half. Shape each half into a smooth, round loaf. Place loaves into prepared pans and press down evenly until dough comes to edges of pan. With a floured sharp knife, cut a large cross, about ½ inch deep, in the center of each loaf. Bake for 35 to 40 minutes or until a wooden pick inserted in center of bread comes out clean. *Makes 2 loaves.*

Italian Bread

1 teaspoon sugar
2 cups lukewarm water
1 package active dry yeast
6 cups flour
1 tablespoon salt

Dissolve sugar in ½ cup lukewarm water. Add yeast and let stand for 10 minutes. Stir in 1½ cups lukewarm water. In a large bowl, stir together flour and salt. Add yeast mixture, stirring until dough is well blended. Turn dough out onto a floured surface and knead until smooth and elastic (about 15 minutes). Place in a greased bowl, turning once to grease top. Cover and let rise until double (about 2 hours).

Turn dough out onto floured surface and knead for 5 minutes. Divide dough into 2 pieces. Shape into balls, cover, and let rest for 10 minutes. Shape each ball into a long loaf, pointed at each end, and place on a greased baking sheet. Let rise until double (about 1 hour). Bake at 425 degrees F. for 10 minutes; reduce heat to 350 degrees F. and continue baking an additional 45 to 50 minutes. *Makes 2 loaves.*

Sopaipillas
Mexico

3 cups flour
2 teaspoons baking powder
½ teaspoon salt
2 tablespoons shortening
1 cup warm water
Vegetable oil for deep-frying

In a large bowl, combine flour, baking powder, and salt. Add shortening, cutting it in with a pastry blender until mixture is crumbly. Add water, a little at a time, to form a pastry-like dough. Turn dough out onto a lightly floured board; cover with a damp cloth and let rest 1 hour.

In a large, heavy frying pan, pour oil to a depth of 1½ inches. Heat oil to 425 degrees F. Divide dough in half. Roll each ball of dough as thin as possible. Cut into 3-inch squares and fry in the hot oil. As they are cooking, gently push squares down into the oil several times so that they will puff evenly. Turn once to brown and cook until golden on both sides. Drain on paper towels. Serve warm with honey. *Makes about 30.*

Pulla Yeast Coffee Bread
Finland

1 package active dry yeast
½ cup warm water
2 cups milk, scalded and cooled to lukewarm
1 cup sugar
1 teaspoon salt
1 teaspoon cardamom
4 eggs, beaten
8 to 9 cups flour
½ cup melted butter
1 egg, beaten
½ cup sliced almonds (optional)
½ cup coarsely crushed sugar cubes
   (optional)

In a large mixing bowl, dissolve yeast in the warm water. Stir in milk, sugar, salt, cardamom, 4 eggs, and 2 cups of the flour. Beat until smooth and elastic. Add 3 more cups flour and beat well. Add melted butter and stir well. Beat until dough looks glossy. Stir in enough of the remaining flour to form a stiff dough. Let rest 15 minutes. Knead until smooth and satiny. Place in a lightly greased mixing bowl and turn to grease the top. Let rise in a warm place until double in size, about 1 hour.

Punch dough down and turn it out onto a lightly floured board. Divide into 3 parts; then divide each of the parts into 3 pieces. Roll each piece into a 16-inch-long rope. Braid 3 ropes together into a long loaf, pinch the ends together, and tuck under. Repeat with the other portions. Lift the 3 braids onto greased baking sheets. Let rise 20 minutes or until puffy but not doubled in size.

Glaze the loaves by brushing with the 1 beaten egg, and sprinkle with almonds and crushed sugar. Bake in a 350 degree F. oven for 25 to 30 minutes or until golden brown. Do not overbake. *Makes 3 large loaves.*

Tea Biscuits
England

2 cups flour
4 teaspoons baking powder
½ teaspoon salt
⅓ cup cold shortening
⅔ cup grated cheddar cheese (optional)
⅔ cup milk

Preheat oven to 450 degrees F. Sift flour, baking powder, and salt together into a large bowl. Cut in shortening with a pastry blender until mixture is the size of large peas. Stir in cheese, if desired. Make a well in the center of the flour mixture, pour in milk, and stir until moistened. Turn dough out onto a floured board and knead gently until well blended. Pat out to 1-inch thickness. Cut with cookie or biscuit cutter and place on ungreased cookie sheets. Bake in preheated oven for about 12 minutes. *Makes 24.*

Bolillos (Yeast Rolls) *Mexico*

2 cups water
2 tablespoons butter or margarine
2 teaspoons salt
1½ teaspoons sugar
1 package active dry yeast
5 to 6 cups flour
1 teaspoon cornstarch
½ cup water

Combine 2 cups water, butter or margarine, salt, and sugar in a small saucepan. Place over low heat and heat just until warm (about 110 degrees F.), stirring constantly. Pour mixture into a large bowl. Add yeast and stir until it is dissolved. Gradually beat in enough flour (about 5 cups) to make a stiff dough. Set dough on a floured board and knead for several minutes, until smooth and satiny. If necessary, knead in more flour to prevent sticking. Place dough in a greased bowl, turning once to grease top. Cover and let rise in a warm place until double (about 1½ hours).

Lightly grease 2 cookie sheets; set aside. Punch dough down and knead briefly on a floured board to release the air. Divide into 16 pieces and shape each piece into a ball. Then gently pull each ball from the center to the ends to make a 4-inch-long roll, the center being thicker than the ends. Place rolls 3 inches apart on cookie sheets. Cover and let rise until almost double in size (about ½ hour). Preheat oven to 375 degrees F. Dissolve cornstarch in ½ cup water in a small saucepan. Bring to a boil over high heat; remove from heat and let cool slightly. Brush mixture over raised rolls. With a floured sharp knife, cut a deep slash about 2 inches long in the top of each roll. Bake for 35 to 40 minutes or until golden brown. Cool on wire racks. *Makes 16.*

Buttermilk Oaten Bread *Ireland*

1½ cups fine oatmeal
1½ cups buttermilk or sour milk
1¾ cups flour
1½ tablespoons sugar
1½ teaspoons baking soda
1 teaspoon salt
½ cup raisins, plumped in hot water and patted dry with paper towel (optional)

If you use "old-fashioned" oatmeal, crush the oatmeal in your hands to refine it. The day before making the bread, mix oatmeal with buttermilk or sour milk in a bowl. Cover; let stand overnight at room temperature.

The next day, sift flour, sugar, baking soda, and salt together into a large mixing bowl. Stir in the oatmeal mixture. Knead with your hands, making a soft ball of dough. Dust with flour if the dough is sticky.

Preheat the oven to 350 degrees F. Lightly flour a baking sheet and set it aside.

Turn out the dough onto a lightly floured surface. Mix in raisins, if desired. Shape dough with your hands into a round loaf 1½ inches thick and 6½ inches across. Cut the loaf into quarters, using a floured butter knife. Cut all the way through, but do not separate the sections. Carefully place on the floured baking sheet and bake for 55 minutes or until well browned. *Makes 1 loaf.*

Farmer's Bread

Poland

2 packages active dry yeast
2 cups warm water (about 110 degrees F.)
1 teaspoon salt
6½ to 7 cups flour
⅓ cup firm butter or margarine,
    cut into small pieces

Dissolve yeast in water in a small bowl. Combine salt and 4 cups of the flour in a large bowl. Cut in butter or margarine with a pastry blender until mixture is crumbly in texture. Add yeast mixture. Stir with a wooden spoon until all flour is moistened. Work in enough additional flour to make a stiff dough. Place dough on a floured surface and knead until smooth and satiny (about 10 minutes), adding flour as needed to prevent sticking. Place dough in a greased bowl, turning once to grease top. Cover and let rise in a warm place until double (1 to 1½ hours).

Lightly grease a large baking sheet. Punch dough down and turn it out onto a lightly floured surface. Knead briefly to release air. Shape into an oval loaf about 7 x 9 inches and place loaf on the baking sheet. Cover and let rise in a warm place until almost double (about 45 minutes). Preheat oven to 400 degrees F. Cut a ½-inch-deep cross in top of loaf with a floured sharp knife. Brush loaf lightly with water. Bake for 25 minutes. Reduce heat to 350 degrees F. and bake bread for about 15 minutes more or until loaf sounds hollow when tapped. Cool on a wire rack. *Makes 1 loaf.*

Pictured on page 29

Focaccia

Italy

2½ cups flour
1 package active dry yeast
2½ teaspoons crushed oregano leaves
½ teaspoon salt
1 cup very warm water (120 to 130 degrees F.)
2 tablespoons olive oil
1 egg, beaten
¼ cup olive oil
Choice of toppings: herbs, cheeses, nuts,
    and vegetables

Combine 1½ cups of the flour, yeast, oregano, and salt in a large bowl. Stir in very warm water and 2 tablespoons oil. Add beaten egg. Stir in enough remaining flour to make a stiff batter. Cover and let rest 10 minutes. Brush a 13 x 9-inch baking pan with olive oil. With lightly oiled hands, spread batter into pan. Drizzle with ¼ cup olive oil and add toppings. Some suggestions: Parmesan or Romano cheese, thinly sliced red onions, pecans, walnuts, rosemary, thyme, garlic. Focaccia is easy to adapt to your individual taste. Cover loosely with plastic wrap; let rise until almost double (about ½ hour). Bake at 400 degrees F. for 25 minutes or until golden brown. Let cool in pan on wire rack or serve warm, cut into squares. *Serves 6.*

Oven Pancake

Germany

3 eggs
½ cup milk
½ cup flour
¼ teaspoon salt
2½ tablespoons butter

In a medium bowl, beat eggs until thick and lemon colored. Add milk, flour, and salt. Mix well. Melt butter in a 10-inch, oven-safe frying pan. Pour batter into the pan of melted butter. Bake at 450 degrees F. for 15 to 20 minutes, until golden brown. Cut in fourths. *Serves 4.*

From top: Seeded Challah (page 34), Hot Cross Buns (page 32), Focaccia (page 28), Corn Bread (page 31)

Corn Bread

¾ cup cornmeal
¾ cup flour
1 tablespoon baking powder
1 teaspoon salt
1 teaspoon sugar
1 cup milk
½ cup vegetable oil
3 eggs
1 can (14 ounces) whole kernel corn, drained
1 large onion, chopped
2 jalapeño peppers, chopped
1½ cups grated cheddar cheese
3 slices bacon, cooked and crumbled

Preheat oven to 400 degrees F. Grease an 8-inch square baking dish; set aside. In a large mixing bowl, combine cornmeal, flour, baking powder, salt, and sugar. Beat milk, oil, and eggs together and add to dry ingredients. Stir in corn, onion, peppers, cheese, and bacon until well mixed. Pour into the greased pan and bake for 30 minutes or until golden brown. *Serves 9.*

Easter Bread (Cresca)

1 package active dry yeast
6 tablespoons warm water
4 to 5 cups flour
½ teaspoon salt
½ teaspoon pepper
¾ cup grated Parmesan or Romano cheese
1 cup milk, scalded and cooled to lukewarm
3 eggs, beaten
2 tablespoons olive oil

In a small bowl, dissolve yeast in the warm water. In a large bowl, sift 4 cups of the flour, salt, and pepper together. Stir in the cheese. Make a well in the center of flour mixture; pour in lukewarm milk, yeast mixture, eggs, and olive oil. Blend well. Turn out onto a lightly floured surface. Knead until smooth and elastic, adding flour if necessary to make a stiff dough. Place in a greased bowl, turning once to grease top. Cover and let rise until double (about 1½ to 2 hours).

Punch down; let rise again until double (about 30 to 45 minutes). Turn out onto lightly floured board and knead. Shape into a round loaf to fit into a 10-inch pie pan. Cover and let rise until double (about ½ hour). Brush top of loaf with olive oil. Bake at 350 degrees F. for 1 hour or until loaf sounds hollow when tapped. *Makes 1 loaf.*

Sweet Bread (Massa Sovada)

1 cup peeled, diced potatoes
2 cups boiling water
7½ cups flour
2 packages active dry yeast
2 teaspoons finely shredded lemon peel
1 cup sugar
6 tablespoons butter or margarine
2 teaspoons salt
4 eggs
1½ cups raisins
1 egg, beaten

Cook potatoes in boiling water until tender, about 20 minutes. Drain, reserving 1⅔ cup liquid. Mash potatoes. In large bowl, stir together 2½ cups of the flour, yeast, and lemon peel. In a small saucepan, heat reserved potato liquid, sugar, butter or margarine, and salt until butter melts, stirring constantly. Pour into flour mixture. Add 4 eggs and mashed potatoes. Beat with electric mixer at low speed for 30 seconds, then increase speed to high and beat an additional 3 minutes. Stir in raisins. Work in enough additional flour to make a moderately stiff dough. Turn dough onto a floured board and knead until smooth and elastic, about 8 to 10 minutes. Place in lightly greased bowl, turning once to grease top. Cover and let rise until double (1 to 1½ hours).

Punch dough down. Divide into 3 parts, cover, and let rest for 10 minutes. Shape each portion into a round loaf. Place loaves on greased baking sheets, cover, and let rise until double (about 45 minutes). Brush tops with beaten egg, cover with foil, and bake at 375 degrees F. for 35 to 40 minutes, removing foil for last 15 minutes of baking time. *Makes 3 loaves.*

Hot Cross Buns

Pictured on page 29

1½ cups milk
⅓ cup butter or margarine
5 cups flour
⅓ cup sugar
2 tablespoons yeast
½ teaspoon salt
1 teaspoon cinnamon
½ teaspoon nutmeg
¼ teaspoon cloves
2 eggs
½ cup currants or candied fruit mix
1 egg white, lightly beaten
1½ cups powdered sugar
1 to 2 tablespoons water
½ teaspoon vanilla

In a small saucepan, heat milk and butter or margarine over medium heat, stirring constantly, until mixture is just warm and butter or margarine is melted. In a large mixer bowl, stir together 2 cups of the flour, sugar, yeast, salt, cinnamon, nutmeg, and cloves. Gradually add liquid; beat with electric mixer for 2 minutes. Beat in eggs. With a spoon, stir in currants or candied fruit and enough of the remaining flour to make dough easy to handle. Turn dough out onto a lightly floured surface; knead until smooth and elastic, about 5 minutes. Place in greased bowl, turning once to grease top. Cover and let rise until double (about 1 to 1½ hours).

Punch dough down. Divide into 4 equal parts. Cut each part into 6 equal parts. Shape each piece into a ball. Place about 2 inches apart on greased cookie sheets. Cut a cross on top of each ball with a sharp knife. Cover; let rise until double. Brush lightly beaten egg white over tops of buns. Bake at 350 degrees F. for 15 minutes or until golden brown. Cool slightly.

Mix powdered sugar, 1 tablespoon water, and vanilla until smooth. Stir in additional water if needed. Drizzle over cooked rolls. *Makes 24.*

English Muffins

England

2 cups milk
2 tablespoons vegetable shortening
2 tablespoons sugar
2 teaspoons salt
2 packages active dry yeast
5½ cups flour
Yellow cornmeal

Heat milk and shortening in a small saucepan until mixture is lukewarm and shortening is melted. Pour into mixing bowl and add sugar, salt, and yeast. Add about 2 cups of the flour and beat with an electric mixer for 2 minutes. Add remaining flour gradually until dough is easy to handle. Turn out onto lightly floured surface and knead until smooth, about 5 minutes. Place dough in greased bowl, turning once to grease top. Cover and let rise until double.

Punch dough down; cover and let rest 10 minutes. Sprinkle a large, flat surface with cornmeal and roll dough out ½-inch thick onto it. Cut with biscuit cutter into 3- or 4-inch rounds. Turn rounds upside down on a cookie sheet that has been sprinkled with more cornmeal. Cover and let rise again until double. Cook on medium hot griddle about 15 to 20 minutes, turning often. Serve warm with butter and jam. *Makes 24.*

Freckle Bread

Ireland

1 small potato, peeled and cubed
1 cup water
1 cup dried currants
2 packages active dry yeast
½ cup warm water
2 eggs, beaten
½ cup sugar
½ cup melted butter or margarine
4½ cups flour
1 teaspoon salt
½ teaspoon mace
½ cup light corn syrup
¼ cup water
½ teaspoon vanilla

In a small saucepan, cook potato in 1 cup water until tender. Leave potato in water and mash very fine, adding water if necessary to make one cup mixture. Stir in currants and let cool to lukewarm. Meanwhile, dissolve yeast in ½ cup warm water in a large bowl. Stir in lukewarm potato mixture, eggs, sugar, and melted butter or margarine. Add 2 cups of the flour, salt, and mace, stirring until smooth. Work in enough remaining flour to make a stiff dough. Turn dough out onto a lightly floured surface. Knead until smooth and elastic. Place in a large greased bowl, turning once to grease top of dough. Cover and let rise until double (about 1 to 1½ hours).

Punch dough down; knead several times. Divide dough in half. Shape each half in a greased 8-inch-round cake pan. Cover; let rise for about 45 minutes. Bake at 375 degrees F. for 30 minutes or until golden brown and hollow sounding when tapped.

In a small saucepan, heat corn syrup and ¼ cup water to a boil; reduce heat and simmer for 5 minutes. Remove from heat and add vanilla. Brush over warm loaves. *Makes 2 loaves.*

Pictured on page 29

Seeded Challah

2 cups flour (approximately)
2 tablespoons brown sugar
1 teaspoon salt
1 package active dry yeast
1 cup water
2 tablespoons butter or margarine
1 egg
⅔ cup whole wheat flour
1 teaspoon poppy seeds
1 teaspoon sesame seeds
½ teaspoon fennel seeds
½ teaspoon caraway seeds
⅛ teaspoon celery, cumin, or dill seeds
1 egg yolk
1 tablespoon water

In a large mixer bowl, combine 1½ cups of the flour, brown sugar, salt, and yeast. Heat water and butter or margarine in a small saucepan until very warm (120 to 130 degrees). Add to flour mixture along with egg. Beat at low speed of electric mixer until moistened; then increase speed to medium and beat an additional 3 minutes. Using a spoon, stir in whole wheat flour and enough additional flour to make dough pull cleanly away from sides of bowl. Cover and let rest 10 minutes. Turn dough out onto a floured surface and knead until smooth. Divide dough into 3 equal parts. Roll each part into a 12-inch rope. Braid ropes together; seal ends. Place on a greased cookie sheet, cover, and let rise until double (30 to 40 minutes).

Preheat oven to 375 degrees F. Mix together poppy, sesame, fennel, caraway, and celery, cumin, or dill seeds in a small bowl. Beat egg yolk and 1 tablespoon water together. Brush braid with egg yolk mixture and sprinkle with seeds. Bake for 20 to 25 minutes or until loaf sounds hollow when lightly tapped. Remove immediately from cookie sheet and cool on a wire rack. *Makes 1 loaf.*

Flour Tortillas

3½ cups *sifted* flour
1 teaspoon salt
½ teaspoon baking powder
¾ cup shortening
¾ cup lukewarm milk

Combine sifted flour, salt, and baking powder in a medium bowl. Blend in shortening thoroughly. Gradually mix in enough milk to make a soft dough. Divide the dough into 16 pieces and roll each into a ball. Preheat an ungreased griddle or heavy skillet over medium-low heat. In the palm of your hand, work each ball with your fingers to soften it and shape it into a slightly cupped form (like the cap of a mushroom). Place on a flat surface and roll out to an 8-inch circle. To prevent edges from being thin and broken, roll only the center of the tortilla, then lift and rotate it a quarter-turn. Repeat process until you have tortilla as thin as possible. Place tortilla on heated grill and cook until lightly browned (about 45 seconds). Flip and brown on other side (about 30 seconds). Stack tortillas and cover with a cotton cloth. Serve immediately or, to serve later, let cool under cloth to room temperature, then place tortillas in an airtight container or plastic bag and refrigerate. Reheat in microwave oven. *Makes 16.*

Pumpernickel Bread

Germany

2 packages quick-rise active dry yeast
1¼ cups warm water
1 cup rye flour
1 cup whole wheat flour
¼ cup dark molasses
2 tablespoons cocoa
1 tablespoon caraway seeds
1½ teaspoons salt
1½ cups white flour (approximately)
2 tablespoons cornmeal

Combine yeast and warm water in a large mixer bowl; let stand until softened, about 5 minutes. Add rye and whole wheat flours, molasses, cocoa, caraway seeds, and salt. Beat mixture with a electric beater until mixed very well.

Add 1 cup of white flour and mix well. Turn out on a floured board and knead until the dough is smooth and elastic, using as little additional flour as possible. Place the dough on a floured surface and cover with a stainless-steel bowl. Allow the dough to rise until double in bulk, about 1 hour.

Sprinkle cornmeal in the center of a cookie sheet and set aside. Punch down the dough and knead it into a ball. Place the dough on the cornmeal and press to form a 6-inch round. Let rise until almost double, about 30 minutes.

Preheat oven to 350 degrees F. Sprinkle a bit of additional flour on top of the loaf. Bake in preheated oven for about 30 minutes or until the loaf is a rich, dark brown and the bottom sounds hollow when tapped. Transfer to a cooling rack. Serve warm or at room temperature. *Makes 1 loaf.*

Peanut Butter Bread

England

2 cups flour
½ cup sugar
4 teaspoons baking powder
1 teaspoon salt
1 cup peanut butter
2 eggs
1 cup milk
¼ cup vegetable oil

Preheat oven to 350 degrees F. Line an 8 x 4-inch loaf pan with waxed paper; set aside. Sift together flour, sugar, baking powder, and salt into a large bowl. Add peanut butter and rub ingredients between fingers until mixture is crumbly. In a small bowl, beat the eggs and stir the milk and oil into them. Pour egg mixture into the flour mixture and stir, scraping bowl often, until thoroughly mixed. Pour mixture into lined loaf pan and bake for 1 hour in preheated oven. Cool on wire rack. *Makes 1 loaf.*

BEEF, PORK, AND LAMB

Beef Noodles
Thailand

3 black mushrooms
2 cups hot water
¼ cup chicken broth or water
1½ teaspoons cornstarch
3 tablespoons vegetable oil
1 pound sirloin tip steak, thinly sliced
½ medium onion, thinly sliced
1 clove garlic, minced
2 cups fresh or frozen chopped broccoli
1 teaspoon fish sauce
1 teaspoon soy sauce
⅛ teaspoon pepper
Cooked rice noodles or egg noodles

In a small bowl, soak black mushrooms in hot water for 15 minutes. Use a colander to drain the mushrooms well; then shred them, discarding the stems. Meanwhile, in another small bowl, dissolve the cornstarch in the broth or water. Set aside.

In a large skillet or wok, heat 2 tablespoons of the oil over high heat for 1 minute. Add meat and cook, stirring constantly, for 2 to 3 minutes or until beef is mostly browned. Remove the meat from the pan and set it aside. Wash skillet or wok and dry thoroughly, then add remaining 1 tablespoon oil and heat over high heat for 1 minute. Stir-fry onion and garlic in hot oil for 2 minutes or until nearly tender. Toss broccoli with onion and garlic in wok, mixing well. Stir cornstarch-broth mixture and pour over the vegetables. Cover, reduce heat, and simmer for 2 to 3 minutes or until broccoli is just tender. Stir in shredded mushrooms, fish sauce, soy sauce, pepper, and meat. Cook, uncovered, over medium heat, stirring frequently, until heated through (about 1 or 2 minutes). Serve over cooked rice noodles or egg noodles. *Serves 4.*

Breaded Beef Cutlets
Argentina

¼ cup flour
½ teaspoon salt
¼ teaspoon pepper
¾ cup bread crumbs
¾ teaspoon oregano
1 egg, beaten
1 pound beef roast (preferably eye of round),
    cut into 8 slices
Vegetable oil
Lemon slices (optional)

Mix flour, salt, and pepper, and spread in a shallow dish. In a separate bowl, mix the bread crumbs and oregano. Dredge beef slices in the flour mixture, then dip them in the beaten egg and coat well with seasoned bread crumbs. Pour enough vegetable oil into a large skillet to cover the bottom. Heat the oil for 1 minute over medium-high heat and add beef slices. Cook over medium heat until browned, 4 to 5 minutes on each side. Garnish with lemon slices before serving, if desired. *Serves 4.*

Barbecued Beef

Korea

¼ cup finely chopped green onions
¼ cup soy sauce
2 tablespoons sesame oil
2 tablespoons sugar
1 tablespoon toasted sesame seeds
½ teaspoon black pepper
1 clove garlic, minced
1½ pounds sirloin tip steaks, thinly sliced into
  ½- by 2-inch pieces
12 romaine lettuce leaves (optional)
1 cup cooked rice (optional)
⅛ teaspoon cayenne pepper (optional)

Combine green onions, soy sauce, sesame oil, sugar, sesame seeds, black pepper, and garlic in a large bowl. Add meat and mix well. Cover and refrigerate 1 to 2 hours. Preheat oven to broil. Lay strips on broiler pan and broil for 2 to 3 minutes per side or until brown. Serve as is or, if desired, place strips of meat on a lettuce leaf with 2 teaspoons hot rice and a dash of cayenne pepper. Roll up leaf. *Serves 6.*

Meat Pies (Lihapiirakat)

Finland

Dough

2 cups milk
1 tablespoon active dry yeast
½ cup melted shortening
4½ to 5 cups flour
2 teaspoons salt

Filling

2 cups water
½ cup pearl barley
1 pound lean ground beef
1½ cups chopped onion
2 tablespoons water
1 beef bouillon cube
1 teaspoon white pepper
1 teaspoon onion powder
2 teaspoons dried dill weed (not seeds)
Salt and pepper to taste
Vegetable oil

To make dough: Scald the milk and let it cool to lukewarm. Add the yeast to the lukewarm milk, stirring to dissolve. Add melted shortening to milk mixture. In a large mixing bowl, sift flour and salt. Add milk mixture to flour and mix to make a soft dough. Knead well. Cover with a towel and let rise for 1 hour.

To make filling: Bring 2 cups water to boil in a small saucepan. Add the barley, cover, and boil for 15 minutes or until barley is tender. Set aside.

In a large skillet, cook ground beef, onions, and 2 tablespoons water until onions are tender. Add bouillon, white pepper, onion powder, dill weed, salt, and pepper. Continue cooking until seasonings are well blended and meat is completely browned. Drain. Add the cooked barley and mix well.

To assemble pies: Roll the dough out very thin on a lightly floured surface. Cut large circles (about 5 inches in diameter) and put a heaping tablespoon full of meat mixture in the middle of each circle. Fold over, moisten edges with water, and seal well around edges. Push down to get all the air out. Let rise for about 30 minutes.

Pour vegetable oil in large frying pan to a depth of about 2 inches. Heat oil to 375 degrees F. Cook pies, 2 or 3 at a time, turning to brown on both sides. Drain on paper towels, then cover with a cloth towel to soften the pies. Cooked pies may be frozen and reheated. *Makes about 20.*

Sukiyaki

1 tablespoon vegetable oil
1 pound boneless top sirloin steak,
    sliced very thin
1 can (10 ounces) bamboo shoots, drained
½ pound fresh mushrooms, sliced thin
1 bunch green onions, cut diagonally
    in 1-inch pieces
1 green bell pepper, cut in strips
4 ribs celery, sliced on diagonal
1 package (10 ounces) frozen French-cut
    green beans, thawed
½ cup soy sauce
¼ cup water or beef broth
2 tablespoons sugar
3 cups cooked rice

Heat oil in a wok or large frying pan. Add slices of meat and stir-fry until well browned. Add bamboo shoots, mushrooms, green onions, bell pepper, celery, and green beans. Mix soy sauce with water or beef broth; stir in sugar. Pour over vegetables and meat in pan. Cook, uncovered, for 5 to 8 minutes, stirring frequently. Do not overcook—vegetables should be tender-crisp. Serve over cooked rice. *Serves 4.*

Braised Flank Steak

1 large flank steak (1½ to 2 pounds), trimmed
    of excess fat
Salt and pepper
1 cup chopped onion
2 small tomatoes, peeled and chopped
¾ cup diced celery
2 cloves garlic, minced
2 tablespoons chopped fresh parsley
2 cups beef broth
1½ cups water
1 teaspoon ground cumin
3 tablespoons vegetable oil

Sprinkle the steak on both sides with salt and pepper. Roll up meat with the grain, then tie tightly with string to hold in a roll, as follows: Tie roll lengthwise, tucking in ends; then tie crosswise at 2-inch intervals. Place in a 13 x 9–inch baking pan. In a medium bowl, mix ½ cup of the onion, tomatoes, celery, garlic, and parsley. Add broth, water, and cumin. Pour over meat. Cover and refrigerate for at least 4 hours or overnight, turning occasionally.

When ready to cook meat, lift the roll from the marinade and pat dry. In a wide, deep kettle, heat 2 tablespoons of the oil over medium heat; add the meat and cook, turning until well browned on all sides. Pour in marinade. Bring to a boil over medium heat; cover, reduce heat, and simmer about 2 to 2½ hours or until meat is tender when pierced with a fork. (Turn meat several times during cooking.) Shortly before serving, heat remaining 1 tablespoon oil in a small frying pan over medium heat; add remaining ½ cup onion and stir-fry until tender. Then lift meat to a serving platter and spoon onions over top. Keep warm. Skim fat from cooking broth; boil over high heat, uncovered, until slightly reduced. Serve meat with broth to be spooned over it. *Serves 6.*

Cabbage Rolls

1 head cabbage
2 pounds lean ground beef
1½ cups cooked rice
1 can (8 ounces) tomato sauce
1 egg
¾ teaspoon allspice
½ teaspoon cumin
½ teaspoon salt
¼ teaspoon pepper
1 to 2 tablespoons vegetable oil

Cut out core of cabbage. Place cabbage in large pot with enough water to cover; boil gently until leaves are tender but not soft. Mix together beef (uncooked), rice, tomato sauce, egg, allspice, cumin, salt, and pepper until well blended. Place a small portion of mixture on each parboiled cabbage leaf and roll up into a roll. Hold together with a toothpick. Heat oil in a large frying pan. Place formed rolls in pan and fry until slightly brown. Place browned rolls in a large casserole dish or Dutch oven, cover, and bake for 1½ to 2 hours at 300 degrees F. *Serves 8.*

Mexican Steak

1 large flank steak (1½ to 2 pounds)
⅔ cup flour
¼ teaspoon salt
¼ teaspoon pepper
¼ cup olive oil
3 tablespoons chopped green bell pepper
2 tablespoons chopped onion
¼ cup chili sauce
2 cups chopped tomatoes (fresh or canned)

Put steak on a bread board or other hard surface and pound the flour into the steak on both sides. Use as much of the flour as you can. Sprinkle both sides with salt and pepper and cut meat into 6 pieces. Heat the oil in a large, oven-safe frying pan over medium-high heat for about 1 minute. Brown steak pieces on both sides in hot oil. Sprinkle the green peppers and onions over the top of the steaks. Add the chili sauce and the tomatoes. Cover and bake at 300 degrees F. for 2 hours, basting frequently with the tomatoes. *Serves 6.*

Rigatoni

3 pounds beef roast (rump, seven-bone, or pot blade)
1 to 2 tablespoons vegetable oil
1 clove garlic, coarsely chopped
1½ teaspoons Italian seasoning
1 teaspoon parsley flakes
½ teaspoon sweet basil
¼ teaspoon salt
⅛ teaspoon pepper
⅛ teaspoon oregano
2 cans (28 ounces each) tomatoes
1 can (6 ounces) tomato paste
1 can (8 ounces) tomato sauce
8 ounces rigatoni pasta
6 ounces Romano cheese, grated

Place roast in a large bowl or pot with enough water to cover. Soak the roast in the water for 1½ to 2 hours. Remove roast from water, trim all fat off, and cut meat into chunks. Return meat chunks to water, squeezing meat until all blood is out.

Coat the bottom of a large roasting pan with oil. Add garlic and brown lightly. Remove most of the garlic, leaving the flavored oil in the pan. Remove meat from water and add to roasting pan. Discard water. Add Italian seasoning, parsley flakes, basil, salt, pepper, and oregano. Cook over medium heat, stirring frequently, until the meat is brown. Add tomatoes, tomato paste, and tomato sauce. Cover and cook on medium heat 1 hour. Turn heat to low and cook for 4 to 5 hours more, adding water if necessary to keep the saucelike consistency. Skim off fat; set mixture aside.

Cook pasta in boiling salted water for about 14 to 16 minutes or until tender but firm. In a 9-inch-square baking dish, put half of the meat sauce, half of the cheese, and all of the pasta. Toss together. Put remaining meat sauce on top and sprinkle with remaining cheese. Heat at 350 degrees F. for 8 to 10 minutes, just long enough to heat through and melt cheese. Serve hot. *Serves 10.*

Stuffed Bacon Rolls   *Belgium*

12 slices bacon
1 medium onion, chopped
2 cloves garlic, minced
1 egg
½ cup tomato sauce
¾ cup soft bread crumbs
1 can (4 ounces) sliced mushrooms, drained
2 tablespoons fresh snipped parsley
¼ teaspoon salt
⅛ teaspoon pepper
1 pound lean ground beef

Partially cook bacon and drain fat off, reserving 2 tablespoons drippings. Return reserved drippings to pan and add onion and garlic; cook, stirring frequently, until onion is translucent. Remove from heat.

In a medium bowl, beat together egg and tomato sauce. Add onion mixture, bread crumbs, mushrooms, parsley, salt, and pepper; combine well. Mix ground beef in thoroughly. Divide into 4 parts.

To make rolls: Place two pieces of bacon on waxed paper, side by side. Cut another slice in half crosswise. Overlapping slightly, place the 2 half slices at one end of bacon slices. Pat ¼ of meat mixture evenly over the bacon. Roll up jelly-roll style, starting from the narrow end. On a rack in a 13 x 9-inch baking dish, place roll seam-side down. Repeat with remaining meat mixture and bacon. Bake at 350 degrees F. for about 40 minutes (longer for well done). *Serves 4.*

Stir-Fried Meat with Sweet Basil   *Thailand*

1 teaspoon dried sweet basil leaves
1 cup hot water
3 tablespoons vegetable oil
1 pound sirloin tip steak, thinly sliced
½ medium onion, sliced very thin
½ cup sliced fresh mushrooms, or 1 can
    (4 ounces) sliced mushrooms, drained
2 jalapeño peppers, seeded and quartered
1 clove garlic, minced
1 tablespoon fish sauce
1 teaspoon sugar

Soak sweet basil in the hot water for 15 minutes. Drain and discard water. Heat 2 tablespoons of the oil in a large skillet over high heat for 1 minute. Add beef slices and stir-fry over high heat until beef begins to turn brown. Place meat in a bowl and set aside. Wash and dry the skillet. Heat remaining 1 tablespoon oil over high heat for 1 minute. Add onion, mushrooms, peppers, garlic, and sweet basil; stir well. Stir-fry over high heat until mushrooms and peppers are tender, about 1 minute. Add beef, fish sauce, and sugar and stir well. Cook, stirring constantly, over medium heat for 2 minutes or until heated through. *Serves 4.*

Baked Steak   *Italy*

1½ pounds round steak, cut about
    ½- to 1-inch thick
Salt and pepper to taste
2 tablespoons apple or grape juice
1 tablespoon Worcestershire sauce
1 can (8 ounces) tomato sauce with cheese
1 small onion, sliced
1 small green bell pepper, sliced

Preheat oven to 375 degrees F. Cut steak into 6 pieces. Season with salt and pepper and place in a shallow baking pan. Sprinkle apple or grape juice and Worcestershire sauce over meat. Pour tomato sauce over and top with onion and pepper. Cover pan with foil. Bake in preheated oven for 45 minutes or until meat is tender. *Serves 6.*

1 teaspoon peppercorns
2 bay leaves
6 whole cloves
2 or 3 juniper berries (optional)
4 cups water
1 cup red wine vinegar
2 teaspoons salt
4 pounds boneless beef roast
 (round or rump)
2 medium onions, sliced
2 ribs celery, sliced
1 carrot, sliced
2 tablespoons vegetable oil
2 slices pumpernickel bread, crumbled
2 teaspoons beef-flavored bouillon granules
⅓ cup raisins
⅓ cup flour
½ cup apple juice

Prepare spices by placing peppercorns, bay leaves, cloves, and juniper berries, if desired, on a 6-inch square of cheesecloth. Gather up corners and tie bag securely. Set aside.

In a medium saucepan, combine water, vinegar, and salt. Add the bag of spices and bring mixture to a boil. Remove from heat and cool to room temperature.

Place meat in a large zip-lock bag with onions, celery, carrot, and bag of spices. Pour vinegar mixture over meat and vegetables in bag and close tightly. Marinate in refrigerator for 3 to 4 days, turning bag over occasionally.

When ready to cook, remove meat from marinade, reserving the vegetables and liquid. (Discard the cheesecloth bag of spices.) Pat meat dry with paper towels. Heat oil in large Dutch oven or kettle; add meat and brown on all sides. Add vegetables from marinade, pumpernickel, and bouillon granules. Pour 3 cups of the reserved marinade over all. Bring to a boil; reduce heat and simmer, covered, for 1½ hours, turning meat occasionally. Add raisins and simmer another 30 minutes or until meat is tender.

Remove meat and vegetables to a serving platter and keep them warm while you make the gravy: Stir flour into apple juice to make a thin paste. Stir into juices in Dutch oven. Cook over medium heat, stirring constantly, until mixture thickens and bubbles; continue stirring and cooking 2 minutes longer. Spoon some gravy over the meat and vegetables and serve the rest in a bowl at the table. *Serves 12.*

Rouladen (Meat Rolls) *Germany*

12 slices beef (top round or top sirloin),
 sliced about ¼ x 4 x 8 inches
1 pound very lean bacon
1 large onion, sliced very thin
¼ teaspoon pepper
Garlic powder to taste
2 to 3 tablespoons olive oil
4 teaspoons low-sodium beef bouillon
 granules
2 cans (14 ounces each) beef broth
4 medium carrots, thinly sliced
1 pound mushrooms, sliced (optional)
2 or 3 bay leaves
¼ cup cornstarch

Place one slice of beef on a flat surface. Place one slice of bacon on top of beef slice. Top with a slice of onion. Sprinkle with pepper and garlic powder. Starting at one short end, roll up beef slice. Hold in place with toothpicks. Repeat with the other slices of meat. In a large roasting pan, heat olive oil. Add the rolls of meat and brown very well on all sides. Add bouillon granules to canned beef broth and pour over rolls to cover. If broth does not cover the rolls, add enough water to mixture to cover them. Add carrots, mushrooms (if desired), and bay leaves. Bring to a boil, then cover and place in oven at 275 degrees F. Simmer for 2 to 3 hours. Remove rolls and vegetables to a serving platter. Discard bay leaves. Add enough cold water to the cornstarch to make a thin paste. Stir the paste into the hot juice in the roasting pan until mixture thickens. Serve over meat rolls. *Makes 12 rolls.*

Meat Loaf with Potato Filling *Italy*

3 teaspoons chopped fresh parsley
2 cups mashed potatoes
1 pound lean ground beef
1 cup plus 2 tablespoons bread crumbs
½ cup water
½ cup grated Parmesan cheese
2 eggs
1 small onion, chopped
Salt and pepper to taste
¼ cup olive oil
½ pound mozzarella cheese, sliced

Blend 1 teaspoon of the parsley with mashed potatoes; set aside. In a large bowl, mix beef, the remaining 2 teaspoons parsley, 1 cup of the bread crumbs, water, Parmesan cheese, eggs, onion, salt, and pepper. Mix well. Brush a 10-inch baking dish with 1 tablespoon of the olive oil; sprinkle with remaining bread crumbs. Place half the beef mixture in dish. Top with mashed potatoes and mozzarella cheese. Place remaining beef on top, sealing firmly around edges to enclose potatoes and cheese. Brush with remaining oil. Bake at 350 degrees F. for 25 minutes. *Serves 6.*

Broiled Steak (Kun Koki) *Korea*

1½ pounds flank steak or sirloin tip
¼ cup sliced green onions (including tops)
¼ cup soy sauce
3 tablespoons vegetable oil
3 tablespoons toasted sesame seeds
2 tablespoons sugar
1 clove garlic, mashed
1 slice fresh gingerroot, ¼-inch thick, slivered
¼ teaspoon pepper

Cut meat into 1-inch cubes. Combine green onions, soy sauce, oil, sesame seeds, sugar, garlic, ginger, and pepper in a medium bowl. Stir in meat and allow to marinate for 1 hour at room temperature. Meanwhile, soak 6 bamboo skewers in water so they won't burn when placed on grill. Skewer meat on presoaked bamboo skewers. Broil 3 inches from heat for 4 minutes. Turn and broil 3 minutes on other side. (May be cooked in oven under broiler or on a barbecue grill.) *Serves 6.*

Ground Steak with Onions (Hakkebof) *Denmark*

¼ cup butter or margarine
4 medium onions, sliced thinly
Salt and white pepper to taste
1½ pounds lean ground beef
Flour
1 tablespoon vegetable oil
1 tablespoon butter or margarine
½ cup whipping cream
½ teaspoon Worcestershire sauce
Chopped fresh parsley

Melt ¼ cup butter or margarine in a large frying pan. Add onions and cook over medium heat, stirring frequently, until soft and golden, 20 to 25 minutes. Season with salt and white pepper; keep warm. Shape beef into 6 patties about ½- to ¾-inch thick. Season lightly with salt and pepper; then coat with flour, shaking excess flour off.

In a large frying pan, heat oil and 1 tablespoon butter or margarine over medium heat. When fat is hot, add patties and cook until well browned on both sides and done to your liking (about 4 minutes on each side for medium). Place patties on a serving platter. Drain excess fat from pan, leaving drippings; add cream and Worcestershire sauce and cook over medium heat, stirring to loosen browned bits, until sauce is bubbly and slightly thickened. Spoon onions over meat, pour sauce over all, and sprinkle with parsley. *Serves 6.*

Meatballs with Buttermilk Gravy *Germany*

1 egg
¼ cup milk
¼ cup fine dry bread crumbs
¾ cup finely chopped onion
1½ teaspoons prepared mustard
1 teaspoon salt
Dash of pepper
1½ pounds lean ground beef
1 tablespoon vegetable oil
1 medium onion, sliced thinly
¼ cup flour
¼ teaspoon salt
2 cups buttermilk
Hot cooked noodles or Spaetzle

Beat egg with milk in a large bowl. Stir in crumbs, chopped onion, mustard, 1 teaspoon salt, and dash of pepper. Add meat and mix well. Shape into 30 meatballs about the size of walnuts. Heat oil in a large frying pan. Add meatballs and cook over medium heat until well browned on all sides. Remove meatballs, reserving 2 tablespoons drippings in pan. Cook sliced onion in drippings until tender. Stir flour and ¼ teaspoon salt into buttermilk until smooth. Add buttermilk mixture to frying pan and cook, stirring constantly, until gravy thickens and bubbles. Reduce heat, return meatballs to pan, and cook 2 minutes more. Serve over hot cooked noodles or Spaetzle (see recipe on page 81). *Serves 6.*

Roast Beef with Roast Potatoes and Yorkshire Pudding *England*

3½ to 4 pounds boneless beef sirloin roast, rolled and tied
Salt and pepper to taste
3 tablespoons vegetable shortening
8 medium potatoes, peeled

Preheat oven to 300 degrees F. Season roast with salt and pepper. Place roast on a wire rack in an open roasting pan with the fat side on top. Dot with shortening. If using a meat thermometer, insert into the center of the roast so that the top does not touch the fat. Roast in the middle of the oven for 3½ hours, or until the meat thermometer registers that the roast is done. For rare beef, thermometer will show 130 to 140 degrees; medium, 150 to 160 degrees; well done, 160 to 170 degrees.

Put peeled potatoes into a saucepan and barely cover with lightly salted water. Boil about 10 minutes. Drain potatoes and arrange them around roast that has already been in the oven for some time. Potatoes should cook for at least 45 minutes to 1 hour. Baste often with fat from meat, turning potatoes occasionally during cooking time. Baste again to brown. Serve roast and potatoes with Yorkshire Pudding (recipe follows). *Serves 6.*

Yorkshire Pudding

2 cups milk
1 cup flour
1 teaspoon salt
4 eggs
Pan drippings from beef roast

Using an electric mixer, blend together milk, flour, and salt. Add eggs one at a time, beating well after each addition. Place pan drippings from roast in an 11 x 7-inch baking dish; put on top shelf of oven heated to 425 degrees F. until drippings are very hot. Pour pudding batter over drippings in dish and return dish to oven for 30 minutes. Serve with roast beef. *Serves 6.*

Wiener Schnitzel

Austria

4 veal cutlets
Juice of ½ lemon
1 tablespoon water
1 tablespoon vegetable oil
1 egg, beaten
½ cup flour
¾ cup dry bread crumbs
Salt to taste
2 to 4 tablespoons vegetable shortening

Pound veal cutlets out flat with a meat mallet. Place cutlets in a shallow pan and sprinkle all over with lemon juice. Let sit at room temperature for 15 to 30 minutes. Mix the water, oil, and egg in a bowl. Place flour on a flat plate and bread crumbs on another flat plate. Sprinkle cutlets with salt and dip them into flour on both sides, then into egg mixture on both sides, and finally into bread crumbs on both sides. Let stand for 15 minutes. Heat shortening in a large frying pan. Add cutlets and fry over medium heat for 6 minutes on each side. *Serves 2.*

Veal Cordon Bleu

France

5 ounces veal
1 slice cooked ham
1 slice Swiss cheese
¼ cup cream
Salt and pepper to taste
1 egg, beaten
Bread crumbs
¼ cup vegetable shortening
¼ cup butter
Lemon slices (optional)

Slice veal into 2 equal parts. Flatten with a mallet. Place ham on 1 slice of veal. Place cheese over ham. Press remaining veal slice lightly on top. Brush lightly with cream and add salt and pepper to taste. Dip veal mixture into egg; roll in bread crumbs. Heat shortening in a small frying pan. Add veal and cook on both sides until very lightly browned. Pour off shortening; add butter. Continue frying veal for about 10 minutes or until well browned. Garnish with lemon slices, if desired. *Serves 2.*

Pork Chops Normandy

France

2 tablespoons butter or margarine
1 tablespoon olive oil
4 pork chops, about 1 inch thick
1 clove garlic, minced
1 medium onion, thinly sliced
1¼ cups apple cider
¼ teaspoon nutmeg
1½ teaspoons salt
Dash of pepper
1 tart apple, peeled, cored, and cut into
    ¼-inch-thick slices
2 tablespoons brown sugar
3 tablespoons light cream

In a large skillet, heat butter or margarine and oil over medium-high heat for 1 minute. Add chops and brown quickly on both sides. Reduce heat to medium-low and cook chops 6 minutes on each side. Remove chops from skillet and place on a serving platter. Pour off all but about 3 tablespoons of the drippings from the skillet. Add garlic and onion to skillet and cook, stirring frequently, until onions are tender but not browned (about 5 minutes). Stir in apple cider, cover, and simmer for 5 minutes. Return pork chops to the skillet. Sprinkle with nutmeg, salt, and pepper. Arrange apple slices over pork chops and sprinkle brown sugar over the top of the chops and apples. Cover and simmer for 15 to 20 minutes or until chops and apples are tender. Stir cream into the skillet with a whisk. Simmer, uncovered, for 5 more minutes. Spoon apple slices and sauce over pork chops to serve. *Serves 4.*

Pineapple-Glazed Spareribs

Pacific Islands

1 slab (about 2½ pounds) pork spareribs
1 can (8 ounces) tomato sauce
1 can (8 ounces) crushed pineapple in juice
⅓ cup vinegar
2 tablespoons light molasses
1 tablespoon prepared mustard
1 teaspoon chili powder
1 teaspoon liquid wood smoke flavoring
1 teaspoon garlic salt or seasoned salt
2 dashes hot pepper sauce

Place spareribs in a large pan with a few inches of water; cover and boil for 30 minutes. Remove from stove and let ribs cool enough to handle. Cut into serving-size pieces. Combine tomato sauce, pineapple with juice, vinegar, molasses, mustard, chili powder, liquid smoke, garlic or seasoned salt, and hot pepper sauce. Pour sauce over ribs, turning ribs to coat with glaze. Cover and let stand for 1 hour. Grill ribs over hot coals or under broiler, brushing occasionally with glaze, until brown and tender. If cooking under broiler, cook for 20 to 25 minutes, turning and basting often. *Serves 4.*

Stir-Fried Pork and Vegetables

Taiwan

2 to 3 tablespoons vegetable oil
1 pound pork tenderloin, cut in thin strips
2 cups chopped onions
3 tablespoons soy sauce
1 teaspoon sugar
1 tablespoon chopped fresh gingerroot
½ head Chinese cabbage, finely shredded
3 green bell peppers, cut in thin strips
Salt to taste
1 tablespoon cornstarch
1 tablespoon water
Hot cooked rice, boiled noodles,
    or fried noodles

Heat oil in a large frying pan or wok over medium-high heat. Add pork and stir-fry until well cooked. Add onions; sauté slightly. Add soy sauce, sugar, and ginger and stir well. Add cabbage and green peppers; stir-fry until heated through but still crisp. Add salt to taste. Mix cornstarch with water and stir into mixture until thickened. Serve at once over rice, boiled noodles, or fried noodles. *Serves 6.*

Italian-Style Pork Chops

Italy

½ teaspoon salt
⅛ teaspoon pepper
1 clove garlic, minced
4 pork chops, about 1 inch thick
1½ tablespoons olive oil
½ cup tomato sauce
¼ cup tomato juice
1 green bell pepper, cut in thin strips
¼ pound fresh mushrooms, sliced, or 1 can
    (4 ounces) mushroom pieces, drained
¾ teaspoon oregano
4 ounces chorizo or hot Italian sausage
    (optional)

Mix salt, pepper, and garlic. Trim excess fat from pork chops and rub salt mixture on them. In a large skillet, heat the oil; add the pork chops and brown on both sides. Add tomato sauce, tomato juice, green pepper, mushrooms, and oregano to the skillet and stir. Cover and cook over low heat for about 30 minutes or until pork chops are tender. Brown sausage (if desired) in a separate pan and drain. Add to the skillet during the last 10 minutes of cooking time. Remove pork chops and sausage from skillet to a serving platter, spoon sauce over chops, and serve. *Serves 4.*

Oven Kalua Pork

Pacific Islands

¼ cup soy sauce
3 tablespoons coarse salt
1 teaspoon Worcestershire sauce
1 small piece fresh gingerroot, crushed,
    or 1 teaspoon ground ginger
1 clove garlic, crushed
5 to 6 pounds boneless pork roast
1 teaspoon liquid wood smoke flavoring

In a small bowl, combine soy sauce, salt, Worcestershire sauce, ginger, and garlic. Mix well. Lay 3 sheets of aluminum foil out, one on top of another. Place roast in center of aluminum foil; rub with soy sauce mixture and sprinkle liquid smoke on top. Fold all 3 sheets of aluminum foil over top of roast and secure tightly. Roast at 375 degrees F. for 5 hours. Shred the pork before serving. *Serves 8.*

Baked Ribs

Philippines

6 to 8 pounds pork spareribs, cut in
    individual servings
1 cup sugar
1 cup white vinegar
1 cup pineapple juice
¼ cup soy sauce
2 tablespoons cornstarch

Preheat oven to 450 degrees F. Place spareribs in a large pan and bake for 30 minutes. Pour off fat. In a medium saucepan, combine sugar, vinegar, pineapple juice, soy sauce, and cornstarch. Cook over low heat, stirring constantly, until thick and clear. Pour sauce over spareribs in pan. Cover tightly with aluminum foil and bake at 350 degrees F. for 1 to 1½ hours. *Serves 8.*

Lamb with Honey

Wales

1 teaspoon ginger
1 teaspoon salt
¼ teaspoon pepper
5½ to 6 pounds leg of lamb
½ teaspoon rosemary
6 medium potatoes, peeled and thinly sliced
Salt and pepper
5 tablespoons butter
2 medium onions, thinly sliced
1 cup apple cider or juice
⅔ cup honey
1 tablespoon cornstarch
1 tablespoon water

Preheat oven to 325 degrees F. Line a shallow roasting pan with foil. Mix ginger, salt, and pepper together and rub meat with the mixture. Place roast fat side up in the prepared roasting pan. Sprinkle with rosemary. Bake lamb uncovered in preheated oven for 1 hour.

Meanwhile, grease a 2-quart casserole. Place ⅓ of the potatoes in the dish; sprinkle with salt and pepper and dot with 1 tablespoon of butter. Top with half of the onions; dot with 1 tablespoon more butter. Repeat layers, ending with potatoes dotted with last tablespoon of butter. Cover with foil. Place in oven with roast for last 1½ hours (see below), removing foil for last 30 minutes of baking time.

After lamb has baked for 1 hour, combine cider or juice and honey; pour over meat. Bake 1½ hours more or until meat thermometer registers 160 degrees F. (Baste occasionally with pan juices during cooking time.) Remove meat to serving platter and keep warm. Drain fat from drippings, saving 1 cup pan juices. Blend cornstarch with water in a saucepan. Add the 1 cup pan drippings. Cook, stirring constantly, until thickened; continue cooking and stirring 2 minutes more. Serve with roast and potatoes. *Serves 6.*

Shrimp Jambalaya (page 57)

POULTRY, FISH, AND SEAFOOD

Simmered Chicken

2 tablespoons soy sauce
1 teaspoon sesame oil
1 tablespoon sugar
⅛ teaspoon salt
⅛ teaspoon black pepper
¼ teaspoon crushed red pepper flakes
8 boneless, skinless chicken thighs,
    cut in 1½-inch pieces
1 clove garlic, minced
1 medium onion, chopped
1 green onion, chopped
Sliced carrots (optional)
Diced potatoes (optional)
Soaked black mushrooms, stems removed
    (optional)

Whisk together soy sauce, sesame oil, sugar, salt, black pepper, and red pepper flakes. Stir chicken, garlic, onion, and green onion together in a large saucepan. Pour marinade over and mix well. Cover and refrigerate for 2 to 3 hours to blend flavors. Add carrots, potatoes, and/or black mushrooms, if desired. Simmer, covered, over low heat until chicken is tender (about 1 hour). *Serves 6.*

Chicken Cacciatore

2½ to 3 pounds chicken, cut into
    serving pieces
¼ cup butter
2 tablespoons olive oil
1 onion, finely chopped
½ green or red bell pepper, chopped
2 cloves garlic, minced
1 teaspoon salt
½ teaspoon pepper
½ teaspoon basil
1 cup canned stewed tomatoes with liquid
½ cup tomato juice, chicken broth, or water
Hot cooked rice or pasta (optional)

Brown chicken in butter and oil in a large skillet over medium heat. When pieces are golden brown on all sides, stir in onion, bell pepper, garlic, salt, pepper, and basil. Cook, stirring occasionally, until onion is tender but not brown, about 5 minutes. Add undrained tomatoes and mix well. Bring to a boil. Cover, reduce heat, and simmer for 20 minutes, stirring occasionally. Add tomato juice, chicken broth, or water and simmer an additional 10 minutes. Remove chicken to serving dish and spoon sauce over the top. May be served over cooked rice or pasta. *Serves 4.*

Golden Chicken

Golden Dipping Sauce

½ cup rice vinegar
⅓ cup sugar
½ teaspoon crushed red pepper flakes
1 tablespoon grated carrot

Chicken

½ fresh pineapple
4 boneless, skinless chicken breast halves
1 teaspoon finely grated lemon peel
¼ cup lemon juice
2 tablespoons vegetable oil
1 tablespoon soy sauce
2 cloves garlic, pressed
Snipped fresh parsley, cilantro, or mint leaves

To make Golden Dipping Sauce: In a small saucepan, combine rice vinegar, sugar, and red pepper flakes. Heat to a boil. Stir in carrot and set aside to cool.

To prepare chicken: Remove pineapple from shell and cut fruit into 1-inch-thick spears or chunks. Place chicken breasts in a shallow baking dish. Combine lemon peel, lemon juice, oil, soy sauce, and garlic and pour over chicken. Cover and marinate in refrigerator 15 minutes. Remove chicken from marinade, reserving marinade. Grill chicken 6 inches from heat for 12 to 15 minutes, turning occasionally and brushing with marinade. Brush pineapple with marinade and grill during last 2 minutes of cooking time for chicken.

To serve: Arrange chicken and pineapple on serving plate. Garnish with parsley, cilantro, or mint. Serve with Golden Dipping Sauce. *Serves 4.*

Roast Chicken

1 whole roasting chicken, 3 to 3½ pounds
1 tablespoon oregano
2 cloves garlic
1 lemon, cut in half
½ cup melted butter or margarine
Lemon wedges (optional)
Snipped fresh parsley (optional)

Preheat oven to 350 degrees F. Rinse chicken inside and out under cold running water and pat dry with paper towels. Place oregano, garlic, and lemon halves inside the chicken, and set chicken in a roasting pan. Roast, uncovered, for 1½ to 1¾ hours, basting every 15 minutes with the melted butter or margarine. (Hint: Keep the butter in a pan on top of the stove where you can warm it as needed.) When chicken is tender and golden brown, remove it to a serving platter and let rest for 10 minutes before cutting. Garnish with lemon wedges and parsley, if desired. *Serves 4.*

Yorkshire Chicken

1¼ cups flour
⅛ teaspoon pepper
1½ teaspoons salt
4 chicken legs with thighs attached
2 tablespoons vegetable oil
2 tablespoons butter or margarine
1 teaspoon baking powder
1 teaspoon rubbed sage leaves
3 eggs
1½ cups milk

Preheat oven to 350 degrees F. Stir together ¼ cup of the flour, pepper, and ½ teaspoon of the salt. Coat chicken in flour mixture. In a large frying pan, heat oil and butter or margarine over medium heat. Add chicken and brown on all sides. Transfer chicken and drippings to a 13 x 9-inch pan. Tilt pan to distribute drippings evenly over the bottom. Place in preheated oven.

Stir together remaining 1 cup flour, remaining 1 teaspoon salt, baking powder, and sage. Place eggs in an electric blender with milk and blend; add flour mixture and blend until smooth. Pour evenly over chicken. Bake, uncovered, for 1 hour or until puffy and browned. Serve at once. *Serves 4.*

Cajun Chicken

2 cups water
1 cup uncooked rice
¼ cup margarine
2 tablespoons flour
1 cup milk
Cajun Spice Blend (recipe follows)
1 pound boneless, skinless chicken breasts,
    cut in strips
½ teaspoon tarragon
1 cup hot cooked peas
1 jar (2 ounces) pimientos, diced and drained

Bring water to boil in a medium saucepan. Add rice, reduce heat, cover, and simmer 20 minutes or until rice is tender and liquid is absorbed. Set aside.

In a small saucepan over medium-low heat, melt 2 tablespoons of the margarine. Stir in flour and cook, stirring constantly, for 2 minutes. Stir in milk and ¾ teaspoon Cajun Spice Blend (recipe follows). Continue cooking and stirring until thick. Keep warm.

In a skillet, melt remaining 2 tablespoons margarine over low heat; add chicken strips, tarragon, and remaining Cajun Spice Blend. Sauté until chicken is done.

Gently stir together cooked rice, peas, and pimientos. Arrange on serving platter and pour white sauce over. Arrange chicken on top and serve immediately. *Serves 6.*

Cajun Spice Blend

¼ teaspoon freshly ground black pepper
¼ teaspoon white pepper
¼ teaspoon cayenne pepper
¼ teaspoon garlic powder
¼ teaspoon paprika
¼ teaspoon salt

In a small bowl, combine black pepper, white pepper, cayenne pepper, garlic powder, paprika, and salt. Blend well.

Spicy Stir-Fried Chicken

Malaysia

2 tablespoons vegetable oil
4 small onions, thinly sliced
4 fresh red or green hot chili peppers,
    seeded and thinly sliced
4 boneless, skinless chicken breast halves,
    cut into 1-inch pieces
¾ cup water
2 tablespoons lime juice
2 tablespoons soy sauce
1 tablespoon sugar
1 tablespoon cornstarch
2 to 3 cups hot cooked rice

Heat oil in a large frying pan or wok. Add onions and stir-fry over high heat for 2 minutes. Add chilies; stir-fry 30 seconds. Add chicken and stir-fry for 5 to 10 minutes. In a small bowl, combine water, lime juice, soy sauce, sugar, and cornstarch. Stir well and add to frying pan. Cook over medium heat, stirring constantly, until thickened and bubbly. Cook and stir 2 minutes longer. Serve over hot cooked rice. *Serves 4.*

Oven-Fried Chicken and Rice *United States—Creole*

¼ cup margarine
½ cup flour
1½ teaspoons paprika
¼ teaspoon poultry seasoning
⅛ teaspoon pepper
2½ to 3 pounds chicken, cut into
   serving pieces
2½ cups chicken bouillon
1 can (16 ounces) tomatoes with liquid
Salt and pepper to taste
1 cup uncooked rice
1 cup chopped celery
½ cup chopped onion
¼ cup to ½ cup chopped green bell pepper
1 clove garlic, crushed
2 tablespoons chopped fresh parsley

Preheat oven to 400 degrees F. Melt margarine in a 13 x 9-inch pan. Mix flour, paprika, poultry seasoning, and pepper, and put into a plastic bag. Drop chicken pieces, one at a time, into the bag and shake to coat. Place chicken skin side down in the melted margarine in pan. Bake uncovered for 25 to 30 minutes or until lightly browned.

While chicken is baking, combine the chicken bouillon, tomatoes with liquid, salt, and pepper in a large saucepan and bring to a boil. When chicken is browned, remove pan from oven and remove chicken from pan. (Do not discard liquid from pan.) Stir together uncooked rice, celery, onion, green pepper, garlic, and parsley; sprinkle over bottom of chicken pan. Lay chicken pieces, skin side up, over the top of the rice mixture. Pour the tomato-broth mixture over the chicken and return pan to oven. Bake uncovered for 40 to 45 minutes longer or until chicken is tender, rice is fluffy, and most of the liquid is absorbed. If necessary, add a bit of broth or hot water during the baking to prevent dryness. *Serves 6.*

Walnut Chicken *China*

1 cup walnuts, coarsely broken
¼ cup vegetable oil
4 boneless, skinless chicken breast halves,
   cut in very thin strips
½ teaspoon salt
1 medium onion, thinly sliced
1½ cups sliced celery
1¼ cups chicken broth
1 tablespoon sugar
1 tablespoon cornstarch
¼ cup soy sauce
2 tablespoons water
1 can (6 ounces) bamboo shoots, drained
1 can (6 ounces) sliced water chestnuts,
   drained
3 cups hot cooked rice

In a large frying pan, toast walnuts in hot oil, stirring constantly. Remove nuts to a paper towel. Put chicken into oil in pan; sprinkle with salt. Cook, stirring frequently, for 5 to 10 minutes or until chicken is tender. Remove chicken and set it aside. Put onion, celery, and ½ cup of the chicken broth in skillet. Cook, uncovered, 5 minutes or until slightly tender. Combine sugar, cornstarch, soy sauce, water, and remaining chicken broth. Pour over vegetables in skillet. Cook and stir until sauce thickens. Add chicken, bamboo shoots, water chestnuts, and walnuts. Heat through. Serve over hot cooked rice. *Serves 6.*

Chicken Sauté

France

2½ to 3 pounds chicken, cut into
    serving pieces
2 tablespoons butter or margarine
1 tablespoon olive oil
⅓ cup flour
½ teaspoon salt
¼ teaspoon thyme
¼ teaspoon pepper
½ teaspoon thyme
1 bay leaf, finely crumbled
2 cloves garlic, chopped
1½ cups canned chicken broth
1 can (3 ounces) sliced mushrooms,
    drained (optional)

Wash chicken pieces under cold running water and pat dry with paper towels. In a large frying pan or heavy kettle, heat butter or margarine and oil. Mix together flour, salt, ¼ teaspoon thyme, and pepper, and place in a plastic bag. Place chicken pieces in the bag, one at a time, and shake to coat. Add chicken pieces to hot oil in pan and brown on both sides over medium-high heat. Reduce heat to low, cover, and cook for 20 minutes, turning chicken twice during cooking time. Sprinkle chicken pieces with ½ teaspoon thyme, bay leaf, and garlic. Slowly pour chicken broth and mushrooms, if desired, into the skillet. Stir gently. Cover the skillet, leaving a small opening for steam to escape through. Cook over low heat until chicken is tender, about 30 minutes. Spoon sauce over chicken pieces to serve. *Serves 4.*

Orange-Stuffed Chicken

Israel

1 whole chicken, 2½ to 3 pounds
1 lemon, cut in half
2 teaspoons salt
1 teaspoon garlic powder
2 teaspoons paprika
1 teaspoon chili powder
1 teaspoon coriander
2 oranges
1 cup water
2 onions, peeled and cut in half

Preheat oven to 425 degrees F. Rinse chicken inside and out under cold running water, pat dry with paper towels, and place in roasting pan. Rub one lemon half over the surface of the chicken. Combine salt, garlic powder, paprika, chili powder, and coriander; sprinkle over chicken. Squeeze juice from remaining lemon half and from 1 of the oranges into roasting pan and add water and onion halves. Place the remaining orange, whole and unpeeled, in cavity of chicken. Cook chicken for 15 minutes, then baste with the pan juices and lower oven temperature to 350 degrees F. Continue cooking chicken for 1 hour and 45 minutes, basting occasionally. Before serving chicken, remove orange from the cavity; cut orange and onions into small pieces and serve with chicken. *Serves 4.*

Rock Cornish Hens

France

6 Rock Cornish game hens
½ cup butter
1½ teaspoons garlic salt
1½ teaspoons crumbled dry parsley leaves
1½ teaspoons salt
1 teaspoon crumbled rosemary
¼ teaspoon white pepper
1 large onion, finely chopped

Preheat oven to 400 degrees F. Arrange hens in lightly greased, shallow baking dish. Melt butter in a small saucepan; add garlic salt, parsley, salt, rosemary, and white pepper. Mix well. Brush mixture over each hen; sprinkle with onion. Bake for 1 to 1½ hours, or until fork tender, basting often. *Serves 6.*

Chicken Curry with Fruit

India

3 pounds chicken, cut into serving pieces
Flour
½ cup vegetable oil
¼ cup chopped onion
1 apple, chopped
4 tablespoons hot curry powder (regular curry may be used, according to taste)
½ teaspoon garlic salt
¼ cup peanuts
Salt and pepper to taste
1 cup buttermilk
½ cup fresh or canned pineapple chunks
1 banana, sliced
3 cups hot cooked rice
Cocktail cherries
Green grapes

Coat chicken pieces with flour and set aside. Heat oil in a large frying pan; add onion and sauté until clear. Add apple, reduce heat, and simmer, stirring occasionally, until tender. Stir in curry powder and garlic salt. Simmer for 5 minutes; then add peanuts. Scoop mixture out of pan with a slotted spoon, leaving drippings. Raise heat to medium-high and fry flour-coated chicken pieces for 20 minutes or until browned on all sides. Season with salt and pepper. Add curry mixture and buttermilk; stir to blend. Add pineapple and banana; heat thoroughly and serve over rice. Garnish with cherries and grapes. *Serves 6.*

Chicken and Peas

Chile

2 tablespoons vegetable oil
3 pounds chicken, cut into serving pieces
5 large potatoes, peeled and quartered
3 carrots, peeled and sliced
1 onion, diced
1 cup water (or more, if needed)
1 or 2 chicken bouillon cubes
1 teaspoon vinegar
4 or 5 whole black peppercorns
½ teaspoon cumin
½ teaspoon paprika
¼ teaspoon oregano
¼ teaspoon seasoned salt
¼ teaspoon garlic powder
Salt to taste
1 bay leaf
1½ cups fresh or frozen peas

Heat oil in a large kettle. Fry the chicken in the kettle until browned on all sides. Remove chicken to a plate, reserving drippings in kettle, and set aside. Add potatoes, carrots, and onion to drippings in kettle and sauté 3 to 5 minutes. Combine 1 cup water, bouillon cubes, and vinegar; pour over the vegetables. Place chicken pieces over vegetables in kettle. Combine peppercorns, cumin, paprika, oregano, seasoned salt, garlic powder, salt, and bay leaf; sprinkle over the contents in the kettle. Cook, covered, over low heat for ½ hour, adding more water if needed. Add the peas and cook 5 to 10 minutes longer or until chicken is done. *Serves 6.*

Almond Chicken

¾ cup blanched whole almonds
3 pounds chicken, cut into serving pieces
¼ cup vegetable oil
½ cup crushed pineapple with juice
1 cup seedless grapes
2 cups orange juice
2 tablespoons honey
⅛ teaspoon ground cloves
⅛ teaspoon cinnamon
⅛ teaspoon thyme

Spread the almonds in a single layer on a baking sheet and toast at 300 degrees F. for 30 minutes, stirring frequently. Cool. Grind ½ cup of the almonds in a blender until fine. Coarsely chop the remaining ¼ cup. Set aside.

In a large frying pan, brown the chicken in hot oil 10 minutes on each side. Arrange pieces in a shallow glass baking dish.

Preheat the oven to 325 degrees F. In a medium bowl, combine the pineapple with juice, grapes, orange juice, honey, cloves, cinnamon, thyme, and ½ cup ground almonds. Pour over the chicken and bake, uncovered, for 40 minutes, basting several times. Increase oven temperature to 350 degrees F., sprinkle the remaining ¼ cup almonds on top of chicken, and bake 10 minutes longer. *Serves 6.*

Pictured on page 48

Chicken Colombiana

2 tablespoons butter
2 tablespoons shortening
3 pounds chicken, cut into serving pieces
⅔ cup flour
¾ cup chopped onion
1 clove garlic, finely minced
½ cup chopped green or red bell pepper
½ cup finely diced carrot
½ cup diced celery
1 tablespoon salt, or to taste
½ teaspoon coarsely ground black pepper
1 teaspoon cumin
2 cups chopped Roma tomatoes
¾ cup chopped, pimiento-stuffed green olives
¾ cup corn (kernels cut off the cob or thawed from frozen)

Heat the butter and shortening in a large frying pan. Coat the chicken pieces in flour and brown on all sides in the hot butter. Transfer the browned chicken pieces to a glass baking dish or Dutch oven, reserving drippings in frying pan. Add onion, garlic, bell pepper, carrot, and celery to the drippings in frying pan; stir-fry 2 to 3 minutes. Spoon the vegetables over the chicken and add salt, pepper, cumin, and tomatoes. Cover and bake at 325 degrees F. for 50 minutes. Add olives and corn. Cook an additional 10 minutes, or until chicken is fork tender. *Serves 6.*

Chicken a la Kieff *Russia*

Chicken

4 boneless, skinless chicken breast halves
Salt and pepper to taste
3 eggs, beaten
1 to 1½ cups bread crumbs
¼ cup butter
½ pound mushrooms, sliced
½ medium onion, diced
2 teaspoons chopped fresh parsley
1 clove garlic, minced

Sauce

¼ cup butter
¼ cup flour
2 cups chicken broth
1 tablespoon Worcestershire sauce
1 teaspoon prepared mustard
Salt and pepper to taste

Pound chicken breasts flat with mallet and season with salt and pepper. Place beaten eggs in a bowl and bread crumbs in another bowl. Melt butter in a large frying pan. Dip chicken in egg and roll in bread crumbs, then dip in egg again and roll in bread crumbs again. Fry in melted butter over medium heat until brown on each side and no longer pink in the middle. Remove chicken from frying pan and set aside. Add mushrooms, onion, parsley, and garlic to the skillet and sauté for 3 to 5 minutes. Pour mushroom mixture into a bowl and set aside. Prepare sauce in same pan: Melt butter and add flour. Add chicken broth and cook slowly, stirring constantly, until thick. Stir in Worcestershire sauce and mustard; season to taste with salt and pepper. Stir until well blended. Return chicken to sauce and top with mushroom mixture; heat through. *Serves 4.*

Curried Turkey *India*

6 tablespoons margarine
1 medium onion, minced
2 tablespoons diced green bell pepper
¼ cup flour
1½ cups turkey broth
1 can (8 ounces) sliced mushrooms, drained
3 cups cubed, cooked turkey
1 large apple, peeled and diced
1 can (8 ounces) sliced water
    chestnuts, drained
3 tablespoons chopped pimiento
1 tablespoon finely chopped fresh parsley
1½ teaspoons curry powder
Salt and pepper to taste
Hot cooked rice

Melt margarine in a large skillet; add onion and green pepper. Sauté until soft. Stir in flour until smooth. Add broth and mushrooms; cook, stirring constantly, until mixture thickens. In a medium bowl, combine turkey, apple, water chestnuts, pimiento, parsley, curry powder, salt, and pepper. Stir well and add to sauce in pan. Heat thoroughly. Serve with rice. *Serves 6.*

Pictured on page 47

Shrimp Jambalaya

United States—Cajun

2 tablespoons butter or margarine
½ cup sliced celery
½ cup chopped green or red bell pepper
½ cup chopped onion
½ teaspoon finely chopped fresh garlic
½ cup uncooked long-grain rice
1 cup cubed, cooked chicken
1 cup water
1 can (16 ounces) tomatoes with liquid
½ pound smoked sausage, cooked and
   cut in ¼-inch slices
1½ teaspoons chicken bouillon granules
½ teaspoon paprika
⅛ teaspoon thyme
⅛ teaspoon cayenne pepper
⅛ teaspoon black pepper
1 small bay leaf
½ pound fresh or frozen raw shrimp,
   shelled, deveined, and rinsed
Hot pepper sauce

Melt butter or margarine in a 3-quart saucepan; add celery, bell pepper, onion, and garlic. Cook, stirring occasionally, over medium heat, until vegetables are tender (4 to 6 minutes). Stir in rice, chicken, water, tomatoes with liquid, sausage, bouillon granules, paprika, thyme, cayenne pepper, black pepper, and bay leaf. Over high heat, cook until mixture comes to a full boil. Reduce heat to low, cover, and continue cooking, stirring occasionally, until rice is tender (20 to 25 minutes). Add shrimp; continue cooking until shrimp turn pink (4 to 5 minutes). Remove bay leaf. Serve with hot pepper sauce. *Serves 6.*

Baked Fish

Greece

2 tablespoons olive oil
2 pounds fish fillets (cod, haddock,
   or bluefish)
2 tablespoons lemon juice
½ teaspoon salt
¼ teaspoon pepper
1 medium onion, thinly sliced
¼ cup finely chopped fresh parsley
1 can (8 ounces) whole tomatoes,
   drained and chopped

Preheat oven to 350 degrees F. Coat a 13 x 9-inch baking dish with olive oil. Arrange fillets in baking dish and sprinkle with lemon juice, salt, and pepper. Place onion slices on top of fish and sprinkle parsley over onion. Scatter tomato pieces over parsley. Bake, uncovered, until fish flakes with fork (25 to 30 minutes), basting occasionally with pan juices. *Serves 4.*

Red Snapper with Almonds

Mexico

1 pound red snapper (or any mild, firm fish)
½ cup chopped fresh cilantro
½ cup toasted, finely chopped almonds
¼ cup butter or margarine
Juice of 2 limes
½ teaspoon salt

Preheat oven to 350 degrees F. Cut fish into 4 pieces and arrange in a baking dish. Sprinkle cilantro and almonds over fish. Melt butter or margarine, add lime juice and salt, and pour over fish. Cover with foil and bake until just tender (25 to 30 minutes). *Serves 4.*

Paella

12 mussels, scrubbed and beards removed,
    or 12 small, hard-shell clams
½ cup water
6 chicken legs
Salt and pepper
2 tablespoons olive oil
¾ pound chorizo or linguisa sausage
1 large onion, chopped
1 red or green bell pepper, chopped
2 cloves garlic, minced or pressed
2 cups uncooked long-grain rice
⅛ teaspoon saffron (optional)
½ teaspoon basil
½ teaspoon oregano leaves
1 package (10 ounces) frozen artichoke
    hearts, thawed
4 cups chicken broth or clam juice
    (or combination)
12 large raw shrimp, shelled and deveined
¼ cup frozen peas, thawed

Optional additional ingredients

Scallops
Lobster tails
Oysters
1 can (8 ounces) stewed tomatoes
Baby clams

In a medium saucepan, place mussels or clams and water and bring to a boil. Cover, reduce heat to low, and cook until shells open (5 to 8 minutes). Remove from heat and let cool. Discard any unopened shells.

Sprinkle chicken with salt and pepper. Heat oil in a large frying pan over medium-high heat. Add chicken and cook, turning as needed, until well browned on all sides. Remove from pan and set aside. Remove the casings from the sausage and cut into ½-inch-thick slices. Add sausage to the pan the chicken was cooked in and cook until browned; remove and set aside.

Discard all but 3 tablespoons of pan drippings. Add onion, bell pepper, and garlic to the drippings. Cook, stirring occasionally, until onion is tender. Add rice, saffron (if desired), basil, and oregano. Stir mixture to coat rice with the drippings. Spread the rice mixture in the bottom of a large, shallow baking dish. Arrange the chicken, sausage, and artichoke hearts over the rice.

Pour broth and/or clam juice into a small saucepan and bring to a full boil; pour over rice in baking dish. Cover tightly with foil. Bake at 350 degrees F. for 30 minutes. Remove from oven, uncover, and stir gently to mix ingredients. Arrange the shrimp on top of the rice. Cover and continue baking for 10 minutes or until shrimp turn pink. Uncover and add mussels; scatter peas over top. Cover and bake about 5 minutes more or until mussels are heated through and all liquid is absorbed.

Note: The optional additional ingredients may be added according to your taste. Add the scallops, lobster tails, oysters, and/or tomatoes at the same time as you add the shrimp. Add clams when you put in the mussels. Arrange all ingredients in an attractive manner on top of the rice. *Serves 6.*

Scrod

3 tablespoons butter or margarine
¼ cup flour
Salt and pepper to taste
¼ teaspoon nutmeg
1½ cups milk
3 ounces cheddar cheese, grated
2½ pounds haddock, halibut, or cod, skinned
    and boned
Paprika

Preheat oven to 325 degrees F. Melt butter in a small saucepan; stir in flour, salt, pepper, and nutmeg. Gradually add milk and cook, stirring constantly, over low heat until smooth and thick. Add cheese and cook, stirring, until melted. Set aside. Place fish in a greased baking dish. Sprinkle with salt and pepper. Pour sauce over fish and sprinkle with paprika. Bake in preheated oven for 45 minutes. *Serves 6.*

Crab Casserole

1 cup fine, dry bread crumbs or cracker
    crumbs
1½ cups milk
2 cups lump crabmeat
3 tablespoons melted butter
¼ cup chopped pimiento
1 tablespoon chopped green bell pepper
1 teaspoon chopped chives, or 1 teaspoon
    grated onion
¼ teaspoon salt
Dash of pepper
3 eggs, well beaten

Preheat oven to 350 degrees F. Butter a 1½-quart baking dish and set aside. In a large bowl, soak crumbs in milk. Mix in crabmeat, melted butter, pimiento, bell pepper, chives or onion, salt, pepper, and eggs. Pour into the buttered casserole dish. Set dish in a pan of hot water and bake for about 1 hour. *Serves 6.*

Fish in Banana Leaf

6 fish fillets: sole, flounder, halibut, or salmon
Salt
¼ fresh coconut, grated (about ½ cup)
3 green chilies, seeded and chopped
1 teaspoon coriander
1 teaspoon caraway seeds
1 teaspoon fresh mint leaves
3 cloves garlic, minced or pressed
1 teaspoon cumin
½ teaspoon salt
1 tablespoon sugar
Banana leaves
Vegetable shortening
¼ cup vegetable oil

Clean fish if needed; sprinkle with salt and set in refrigerator. Grind coconut, chilies, coriander, caraway, mint, garlic, cumin, ½ teaspoon salt, and sugar to a paste in a blender or grinder. Coat each side of fish with paste. Wash banana leaves; cut into pieces. Dry with paper towels and grease on one side with shortening. Wrap each fish piece into a square on greased side of leaf. Tie shut with a thread. In a large frying pan, fry fish "packets" in hot oil for 5 minutes on each side. Place in a greased baking dish and bake at 350 degrees F. for 15 minutes.

Note: If banana leaves are not available, spread half the paste in a greased baking dish. Place fillets of top and spread remaining paste on top. Cover dish with lid or aluminum foil. Bake for 30 minutes at 350 degrees. *Serves 6.*

Bangkok Shrimp

2 teaspoons curry powder
⅓ teaspoon celery seed
⅔ teaspoon cumin
¾ teaspoon salt
1 pound shrimp, peeled and deveined
¼ cup butter
Hot cooked rice

In a medium bowl, mix together curry powder, celery seed, cumin, and salt. Add shrimp and toss until well coated with seasonings. Melt butter in a heavy pan; add shrimp and sauté until pink. Serve over hot cooked rice. *Serves 6.*

Shrimp Fra Diavolo
Italy

⅓ cup olive oil
1 medium onion, chopped
2 cloves garlic, minced
1 can (28 ounces) Italian-style tomatoes
2 tablespoons chopped fresh parsley
1½ teaspoons salt
1 teaspoon oregano
1 teaspoon basil
Dash of cayenne pepper
1 package (6 ounces) macaroni or
    spaghetti noodles
2 pounds shrimp, peeled and deveined
¼ cup olive oil

Heat ⅓ cup olive oil in a large frying pan; add onion and garlic and sauté until onion is clear. Add tomatoes, parsley, salt, oregano, basil, and cayenne pepper. Cover and simmer for 30 minutes. Cook macaroni or spaghetti noodles according to package directions. Sauté shrimp in ¼ cup olive oil until pink; add to tomato mixture. Serve over cooked pasta. *Serves 6.*

Fish Poached in Milk
Canada

1 cup milk
½ teaspoon salt, or to taste
4 fish fillets
2 tablespoons butter or margarine
2 tablespoons flour
⅛ teaspoon pepper
1 teaspoon lemon juice
2 tablespoons chopped green onions or
    chopped fresh chives

Heat milk and salt in a medium saucepan; add fish fillets and simmer for 5 to 10 minutes or until fish flakes easily with a fork. Remove from heat. With a slotted spoon, carefully remove fish to heated serving platter and keep warm. Save milk. Melt butter or margarine in a medium frying pan. Stir in flour and pepper. Gradually add the hot milk that the fish was cooked in; cook over medium heat, stirring constantly, until mixture thickens. Add lemon juice and 1 tablespoon of the chopped green onions or chives. Stir well. Pour over fish. Sprinkle with remaining chopped onions or chives. Serve immediately. *Serves 4.*

Red Snapper Vera Cruz
Mexico

3 tablespoons olive oil
1 large onion, thinly sliced and
    separated into rings
3 cloves garlic, minced
8 fresh tomatoes, peeled, seeded, and chopped
2 or 3 canned jalapeños, rinsed and cut
    crosswise in thin slices
1 jar (4 ounces) pimiento-stuffed green olives,
    drained and cut in half crosswise
¼ teaspoon cinnamon
Pinch of cloves
Juice of ½ lemon
½ teaspoon salt (optional)
3 pounds red snapper fillets
1 tablespoon capers
2 tablespoons coarsely chopped fresh cilantro

Preheat oven to 350 degrees F. Heat oil in a medium frying pan; add onion and garlic and sauté until tender. Add tomatoes, jalapeños, olives, cinnamon, cloves, and lemon juice. Reduce heat and simmer about 5 minutes to blend flavors. Taste for seasoning and add salt if necessary. Keep warm.

In a shallow baking pan, place the fish in a single layer and bake in preheated oven until fish flakes easily with a fork (about 15 minutes). Arrange fillets on a heated platter, spoon the sauce over the fish, and garnish with capers and cilantro. *Serves 4.*

Baked Salmon

Canada

1 small, whole salmon (about 4 pounds)
1 teaspoon instant minced onion
1 teaspoon minced dill pickle
½ teaspoon dried parsley flakes
1 cup bread crumbs
¼ cup evaporated milk
2 tablespoons butter
1 teaspoon salt
⅛ teaspoon pepper
½ cup water
1 lemon, cut in wedges

Preheat oven to 350 degrees F. Clean the fish; pat dry with paper towels. In a medium bowl, combine the onion, pickle, parsley, and bread crumbs. Add the milk and let soak. Place the fish in a greased baking dish and stuff with the crumb mixture. Dot the surface with butter and sprinkle with salt and pepper. Add water to the dish and place in preheated oven. Bake, uncovered, about 1 hour, basting the fish frequently with the liquid from the bottom of the dish. (Note: Fish may be baked in a baking bag, if desired.) Serve hot with wedges of fresh lemon. *Serves 6.*

Broiled Salmon Steaks with Lime Butter

Canada

1 cup butter or margarine
2 teaspoons lime juice
2 teaspoons chopped fresh dill weed,
    or ½ teaspoon dried dill weed
¼ teaspoon pepper
8 salmon steaks, cut 1 inch thick
2 limes, each cut into 8 slices

Combine butter or margarine, lime juice, dill, and pepper. Grease a broiler pan and arrange salmon steaks on the pan. Spread top side of each steak with 2 teaspoons lime butter. Broil 5 inches from heat until lightly browned (5 to 6 minutes). Turn steaks over and top each steak with 2 lime slices. Continue broiling until salmon flakes with a fork (5 to 6 minutes). To serve, top each steak with 1 tablespoon lime butter and garnish with lime slices. *Serves 8.*

Baked Halibut

Canada

4 slices salt pork, or 4 strips bacon
1 small onion, thinly sliced
1 bay leaf
2 pounds halibut, cut into 6 pieces
¼ cup buttered bread crumbs
Paprika
Fresh lemon juice
Snipped fresh parsley

Preheat oven to 400 degrees F. Lay the salt pork or bacon on the bottom of a baking dish. Add onion and bay leaf. Arrange halibut over the onions and cover with buttered bread crumbs. Cover with foil. Bake in preheated oven for 40 minutes. Sprinkle with paprika and lemon juice and garnish with parsley. *Serves 6.*

Microwaved Sweet and Sour Fish Fillets

Pacific Islands

1 can (8 ounces) pineapple tidbits in juice
1 tablespoon sugar
1 tablespoon cider vinegar
1½ teaspoons cornstarch
½ teaspoon instant chicken bouillon granules
¼ teaspoon ginger
1 pinch red pepper
¼ cup sliced green onions
¼ cup sliced water chestnuts
4 white fish fillets, cut ½ inch thick
2 tablespoons melted butter or margarine
½ cup bread crumbs
Paprika

Drain pineapple, reserving the juice for the sauce. Add enough water to juice to make ⅔ cup liquid; pour into a microwave-safe bowl. Stir in sugar, vinegar, cornstarch, bouillon, ginger, and red pepper. Microwave on high setting 4 to 5 minutes, until sauce boils and thickens. To prevent lumps, stir after 2 minutes. Stir in green onions, water chestnuts, and pineapple; set aside. In a 12 x 8-inch microwave-safe baking dish, arrange the fish fillets with the thickest parts facing outside edges. Drizzle with butter or margarine, then sprinkle with bread crumbs and paprika. Cover with waxed paper. Microwave on high 5 to 9 minutes, rotating dish after 3 minutes. Fish is done when thin areas flake easily with a fork and thick areas are fork tender. Let fish stand 2 to 3 minutes; then pour pineapple sauce over and serve. *Serves 4.*

Shrimp with Fresh Pineapple

Pacific Islands

½ medium fresh pineapple
¼ teaspoon allspice
¼ teaspoon cinnamon
¼ teaspoon cloves
¼ teaspoon ginger
¼ teaspoon crushed red pepper flakes
¼ teaspoon anise seeds (optional)
1 pound large shrimp, peeled and deveined
½ teaspoon salt
1 teaspoon vegetable oil
1 onion, cut into wedges
1 clove garlic, pressed
1 red bell pepper, sliced
1½ teaspoons cornstarch
¾ cup water
2 tablespoons chopped fresh cilantro
2 tablespoons chopped fresh mint leaves

Cut pineapple from shell and slice crosswise into thin slices. Set aside. In a cup, combine allspice, cinnamon, cloves, ginger, red pepper flakes, and anise seeds, if desired. Mix well. Spread shrimp in single layer on plate; sprinkle with salt and half of the spice mixture. Heat oil in a large frying pan; add onion, garlic, and bell pepper and sauté until tender. Blend cornstarch with water; stir into vegetables in frying pan along with remaining spice mixture. Arrange shrimp on top of vegetables. Reduce heat, cover, and simmer, stirring occasionally, for 5 to 7 minutes or until shrimp are pink. Remove shrimp to serving plate with slotted spoon. Add pineapple to vegetables in skillet with 1 tablespoon each cilantro and mint. Stir until heated through. Place vegetables and fruit with shrimp on platter and serve with remaining cilantro and mint sprinkled over the top. *Serves 4.*

CASSEROLES AND MAIN DISHES

Shepherd's Pie

England

2 quarts water
1 tablespoon salt
3 large potatoes, peeled and quartered
2 tablespoons butter
Salt and pepper to taste
¼ to ⅓ cup milk
1 tablespoon vegetable oil
1 large onion, chopped
1 pound lean ground beef
1 large carrot, grated
1 tablespoon chopped fresh parsley
½ clove garlic, finely chopped,
    or pinch of garlic powder
½ teaspoon thyme
1 tablespoon soy sauce
Grated cheddar cheese (optional)

In a large saucepan, bring water to a boil; stir in salt. Add potatoes and boil them gently for about 15 to 20 minutes or until they are soft. Drain off water and add butter and salt and pepper to taste. Mash the potatoes, adding enough milk to make a smooth mixture. Set aside.

Preheat oven to 375 degrees F. In a large skillet, heat the oil over medium-high heat for 1 minute. Add the onion and stir-fry until tender. Stir in ground beef; then add carrot, parsley, garlic, and thyme. Cook until beef is thoroughly browned, stirring frequently. Drain off any excess oil. Add soy sauce and stir well. Taste, and add more salt and pepper if desired. Spread the meat mixture evenly in the bottom of a deep pie dish. Top with mashed potatoes. Sprinkle with grated cheese, if desired. Bake in preheated oven for 30 minutes or until cheese melts and top is lightly browned. *Serves 4.*

Pictured on cover

Curry

Republic of South Africa

2 to 3 pounds boneless lamb or beef,
    cut in chunks
4 carrots, diced
1 potato, diced
2 cups water
1 teaspoon salt
2 tablespoons butter
3 onions, chopped
½ cup flour
3 tablespoons curry powder
½ teaspoon ginger
1 bay leaf
Salt and pepper to taste
4 fresh tomatoes, chopped, or 1 can
    (14½ ounces) diced tomatoes
1 cup tomato juice or water
6 cups cooked rice
Flaked coconut
Chopped tomato
Chopped banana
Chutney
Raisins
Pineapple

Place beef or lamb in a large kettle with enough water to cover meat; simmer for 2 hours. Cook carrots and potato in boiling, salted water until tender. Drain, reserving ½ cup liquid. In a large pan, melt butter; add onions and cook, stirring frequently, until tender. Add flour, curry powder, ginger, bay leaf, and salt and pepper; stir until blended. Mix in tomatoes and tomato juice or water. Add the cooked vegetables with reserved liquid and meat with the liquid it was cooked in. Cover and simmer for 30 minutes. Serve over cooked rice with the following garnishes: flaked coconut, chopped tomato, chopped banana, chutney, raisins, and pineapple. *Serves 8.*

Ham and Broccoli Crepes with Mornay Sauce

France

Crepes

4 eggs
¼ teaspoon salt
2 cups flour
2¼ cups milk
¼ cup melted butter

Filling

2 packages (8 ounces each) frozen broccoli
    spears, or 1 pound fresh broccoli spears
12 thin slices cooked ham
Butter

Mornay Sauce

1 tablespoon butter
1 tablespoon flour
1 cup milk
3 tablespoons grated Swiss cheese
1 tablespoon grated Parmesan cheese
½ teaspoon mild prepared mustard
    (Dijon style is best)
Salt and pepper to taste

To make crepes: In a large mixer bowl, combine the eggs and salt. Stir in flour alternately with milk, beating until smooth and creamy. Beat in butter. Chill batter in refrigerator for at least 1 hour. Lightly grease a crepe pan or a medium frying pan. Heat the pan for several seconds, lift it off the burner, and pour in 2 or 3 tablespoons of batter. Quickly swirl the batter around the pan so that a thin, even layer covers the bottom. Set the pan back on the heat and cook the crepe over medium heat. When the crepe bottom is brown, carefully flip the crepe over with a spatula. Brown the other side; then remove the crepe from the pan with a spatula. Repeat with remaining batter.

To assemble crepes: In a medium saucepan, cook broccoli spears in lightly salted water until tender (about 10 to 15 minutes). Slice each spear in half. Preheat oven to 400 degrees F. Cover each crepe with a slice of ham. Place 2 or 3 broccoli spears on top of ham and roll up crepe. Place seam-side down in a buttered 13 x 9-inch casserole dish. Dot surface of crepes with butter and bake for 15 minutes.

To make Mornay Sauce: Melt butter in saucepan. Remove from heat and stir in flour with a whisk. Return to medium heat and slowly add milk, stirring constantly until sauce is thickened. Add cheeses, mustard, and salt and pepper.

To serve: Place 2 crepes on each serving plate. Spoon Mornay Sauce over crepes. *Serves 6.*

Family Size Beef Pie

Finland

Crust

1 cup butter or margarine, softened
2 small potatoes, cooked, peeled, and grated
1 tablespoon cold water
1½ cups flour
½ teaspoon baking powder

Filling

½ pound ground beef
¼ cup chopped onion
¼ teaspoon salt
Pepper to taste
2 cups cooked rice
2 eggs, hard boiled and chopped

Other ingredients

1 egg white, beaten
2 cans (14 ounces each) beef broth

To make crust: Mix butter with cold potatoes. Add water. Sift together flour and baking powder and add to mixture. Don't overmix. Chill.

To make filling: In a large frying pan, brown ground beef with the chopped onion. Drain. Add salt and pepper. Mix in rice and chopped eggs.

To make pie: Divide dough into two parts, one a little larger than the other. Roll the bigger piece into a rectangle on a 16 x 11 x 1-inch cookie sheet. Spread filling to within 1 inch of the edges. Roll the rest of the dough out 1 inch smaller around than the bottom crust, and place it on top of filling. Brush edges of bottom crust with water and fold them over the top. Press with fork all around the edge. Brush with beaten egg white and prick with fork. Bake at 425 degrees F. for 20 minutes. To serve, cut into squares and pour beef broth over. *Serves 12.*

Paella (page 58)

Stuffed Manicotti

¼ cup olive oil
1 pound lean ground beef
2 cans (6 ounces each) tomato paste
2 cups water
½ cup chopped onion
1 clove garlic, minced
2 tablespoons chopped fresh parsley
4 teaspoons fresh basil (optional)
1½ teaspoons oregano
1½ teaspoons salt
Dash of pepper
1 pound cottage cheese
⅓ cup grated Parmesan cheese
1 egg, well beaten
2 tablespoons chopped fresh parsley
1 teaspoon thyme
1 teaspoon marjoram
Salt and pepper to taste
8 ounces manicotti
Romano cheese

In a large skillet, heat oil and add ground beef; brown lightly. Stir in tomato paste, water, onion, garlic, 2 tablespoons parsley, basil (if desired), oregano, 1½ teaspoons salt, and dash pepper. Simmer, uncovered, about 45 minutes, stirring occasionally. Meanwhile, in a medium bowl, mix cottage cheese, Parmesan cheese, beaten egg, 2 tablespoons parsley, thyme, and marjoram. Add salt and pepper to taste; set aside. Cook manicotti in boiling salted water until tender; drain and rinse in cold water. Stuff the manicotti with the cheese mixture. Pour half of the tomato-meat mixture into an 11 x 7-inch baking dish. Arrange the stuffed manicotti in a layer on sauce, overlapping slightly. Pour remaining sauce over the top. Sprinkle with Romano cheese. Bake at 350 degrees F. for 25 to 30 minutes. *Serves 8.*

Navajo Tacos

3 cups small uncooked red beans
Water for soaking and cooking beans
1 pound lean ground beef
1 can (8 ounces) tomato sauce
1 package chili seasoning mix
Navajo Fry Bread (recipe follows)
Chopped lettuce
Chopped tomato
Chopped onion
Grated cheddar cheese
Salsa or taco sauce

Soak beans in cold water for at least 2 hours or overnight. Drain beans and place them in a large pot with 5 cups water. Bring to a boil, cover, and cook, boiling steadily, for 1 hour. Reduce heat and cook, covered, for 2 more hours. Crumble beef into pot and cook, stirring frequently, until browned (about 20 minutes). Add tomato sauce and chili seasoning and simmer for an additional 10 minutes to blend flavors.

While mixture simmers, prepare a double batch of Navajo Fry Bread (recipe follows). Spoon bean mixture onto hot fry bread and top with any combination of lettuce, tomato, onion, cheese, salsa, and taco sauce. *Serves 12.*

Navajo Fry Bread

2 cups flour
3 teaspoons baking powder
¾ teaspoon salt
1 cup warm water
Shortening or vegetable oil for deep-frying

Combine flour, baking powder, and salt. Stir in warm water until soft dough forms. (This can be done quickly and easily in a food processor, if desired.) Pinch off a piece of dough the size of a tennis ball. Roll out with a rolling pin or form with hands into a 6-inch circle. Melt shortening or pour oil in a large frying pan to a depth of about 1 inch. Heat to 375 degrees F. Fry bread on both sides until golden brown. Drain on paper towels. Use in Navajo Tacos, or serve with butter and honey or jam. *Makes 6 servings.*

Enchiladas

1½ to 2 pounds lean ground beef
1 onion, diced
2 cups water
2 tablespoons chili powder
3 tablespoons vegetable oil
2 tablespoons flour
1 can (15 ounces) tomato sauce
Salt and pepper to taste
12 soft 6-inch corn tortillas
1 pound cheddar cheese, grated
Grated onion (optional)

Preheat oven to 350 degrees F. Brown ground beef and onions in a large frying pan. Drain and set aside. Combine water and chili powder in a small bowl and set aside. In a large frying pan, heat oil and add flour, stirring until mixture is brown. Slowly add chili powder mixture and continue cooking, stirring constantly, until mixture thickens. Add tomato sauce, salt, and pepper. Stir until well blended. Simmer, uncovered, about 5 minutes. Soften tortillas by heating in microwave or wrapping in aluminum foil and heating in oven. Place some of the meat mixture in each tortilla, top with grated cheese, and roll. Place seam-side down in a baking dish; cover with tomato sauce mixture and any remaining meat mixture, cheese, and grated onion, if desired. Bake for 30 minutes in preheated oven, or until hot and bubbly. *Serves 6.*

Note: 3 cups shredded, cooked beef or chicken may be substituted for ground beef.

Chimichangas

Mexico

2 onions, chopped
2 cloves garlic, minced
1 tablespoon vegetable oil
2 pounds lean ground beef
2 medium tomatoes, chopped
1 can (8 ounces) Anaheim green chilies, chopped
1 teaspoon cumin
½ teaspoon salt
Pepper to taste
½ pound mild cheddar cheese, grated
20 flour tortillas (10-inch size)
Vegetable oil for frying
Salsa
Sour cream

Sauté onions and garlic in 1 tablespoon oil in a large frying pan for 2 to 3 minutes. Add ground beef and cook until thoroughly browned. Remove from heat and drain off excess fat; mix in the tomatoes, green chilies, cumin, salt, and pepper. Place a small amount of grated cheese in the middle of a tortilla. Top with 2 or 3 tablespoons of meat mixture. Fold sides and ends in to middle like an envelope to seal in meat mixture. Secure with a toothpick. Brown on all sides in a small amount of oil in a frying pan. (For a lower fat content, bake at 400 degrees F. for 20 minutes or until brown.) Repeat with remaining tortillas. Put chimichangas under broiler to crisp them. Serve with salsa and sour cream. *Makes 20.*

Note: 3 cups shredded, cooked beef or chicken may be substituted for ground beef.

Breakfast Soufflé

Netherlands

5 eggs
2 cups milk
½ teaspoon dry mustard
½ teaspoon salt
6 slices white bread, cubed
½ pound mild sausage links, cut into ¼-inch pieces
1 cup grated sharp cheddar cheese

Beat together eggs and milk in a medium bowl. Stir in mustard and salt. Place bread cubes in a large bowl; pour milk mixture over them, cover bowl, and let bread soak overnight in refrigerator. Next morning, fry sausages until brown; set aside. (Note: Ham, shrimp, crab, or mushrooms may be substituted for the sausage.) Put bread mixture in a greased 13 x 9-inch pan and arrange browned sausages over top. Bake, uncovered, at 350 degrees F. for 35 minutes. Remove casserole from oven and sprinkle with cheese. Bake an additional 10 minutes. *Serves 12.*

Beef Casserole (Pastitsio) *Greece*

1½ pounds lean ground beef
1 cup chopped onion
1 can (14 ounces) tomatoes, cut up
1 can (6 ounces) tomato paste
1 teaspoon salt
¼ teaspoon thyme
2 cups dry elbow macaroni (7-ounce package)
4 slightly beaten egg whites
½ cup feta cheese, cubed (American cheese may be substituted)
½ cup butter or margarine
½ cup flour
1 teaspoon salt
¼ teaspoon cinnamon
4 cups milk
4 slightly beaten egg yolks

Cook ground beef and onions in a large skillet until the beef is browned; drain excess fat. Add undrained tomatoes, tomato paste, 1 teaspoon salt, and thyme. Cover and simmer for 30 minutes, stirring occasionally to prevent sticking. Cook macaroni according to package directions; drain well. Stir egg whites and cheese into macaroni, then stir in meat mixture and mix well. Pour into a 13 x 9-inch baking pan. Set aside.

In a large saucepan, melt butter or margarine and then blend in flour, 1 teaspoon salt, and cinnamon. Add milk and cook over medium heat, stirring constantly, until mixture is thickened and bubbly. Remove from heat and slowly stir a small amount of the milk mixture into the egg yolks. Blend well. Pour egg yolks back into the hot milk mixture, stirring quickly to mix. Pour white sauce on top of meat mixture. If desired, lightly sprinkle additional cinnamon on top of sauce. Bake at 375 degrees F. until heated through, 35 to 40 minutes. Let stand 10 minutes before serving. *Serves 12.*

Meat and Potato Pie (Pastel de Papas) *Chile*

Potato mixture

10 medium potatoes
1 teaspoon salt
3 tablespoons butter
1 egg
Milk

Meat mixture

2 tablespoons vegetable oil
4 or 5 large onions, finely diced
2 cloves garlic, minced
1½ teaspoons cumin
½ teaspoon oregano
½ teaspoon paprika
¼ teaspoon black pepper
¼ teaspoon cayenne pepper
Salt to taste
1 pound lean ground beef
½ cup raisins
1 can (6 ounces) pitted black olives
4 eggs, hard boiled
Butter
2 tablespoons sugar

Peel and cut potatoes in quarters and place in a 3-quart saucepan. Cover with water and add 1 teaspoon salt. Bring to a boil, reduce heat, and boil gently about 20 minutes or until potatoes are soft. Pour off water and mash the potatoes, adding butter, egg, and enough milk to make a moist but not runny mashed mixture. Set aside.

Heat oil in large skillet. Add onions, garlic, cumin, oregano, paprika, black pepper, cayenne pepper, and salt; cook over medium-high heat until onions are transparent. Crumble ground beef into the onion mixture and continue cooking, stirring frequently, until meat is browned. Remove from heat and stir in raisins and olives. Place meat mixture in a 13 x 9-inch baking dish. Slice eggs and lay slices on top of meat mixture. Cover with mashed potatoes. Dot with butter and sprinkle with sugar. Bake at 400 degrees F. for 30 minutes or until lightly browned. Cut into squares and serve hot. *Serves 10.*

Scalloped Ham and Apples $\qquad$ *Norway*

1 cup brown sugar
1 teaspoon ground cloves
3 cups sliced apples
3 cups cooked, chopped ham
½ cup pineapple juice

Mix brown sugar and cloves together in a small bowl. Place a layer of apples in the bottom of a 12 x 8-inch baking dish. Sprinkle with sugar mixture and top with a layer of ham pieces. Repeat layers until ingredients are used up. Pour pineapple juice over top. Bake uncovered at 300 degrees F. for 1½ hours or until apples are tender when pierced with a fork. *Serves 8.*

Cheese-Filled Pancakes (Nalezniki) $\qquad$ *Russia*

2 cups cottage cheese
2 eggs
1½ cups warm milk
4 egg yolks
1¼ cups flour
4 egg whites
1 teaspoon salt
1 cup cream
½ cup melted butter

In a medium bowl, stir together the cottage cheese and 2 eggs. Mix well and set aside. Place warm milk in a small bowl; beat in 4 egg yolks. Add flour and continue beating until smooth. In a separate bowl, beat egg whites with salt until firm. Fold beaten egg whites into milk mixture.

Heat a large frying pan over medium heat. Ladle ¼ cup of batter onto hot pan and tilt pan to spread batter slightly. Cook pancake on both sides. Place 1 rounded tablespoon of cottage cheese mixture on pancake and roll up. Place roll in a 13 x 9-inch baking dish. Repeat with remaining batter and filling. Mix cream with melted butter and pour over rolls. Bake, uncovered, at 400 degrees F. about 15 minutes or until cream is bubbly. Serve hot. *Serves 8.*

Frittata $\qquad$ *Spain*

3 tablespoons olive oil
1 large potato, peeled and thinly sliced
1 medium onion, thinly sliced
1 large red bell pepper, sliced
Salt and pepper to taste
1 tablespoon chopped fresh thyme, or
   1 teaspoon dried thyme
6 eggs
½ cup grated Parmesan cheese
2 tablespoons chopped fresh parsley
2 tablespoons capers

In a large, nonstick frying pan, heat 2 tablespoons of the oil over medium heat. Place half of the potato slices in the skillet. Place a layer of onion and then bell pepper slices over the potatoes. Season with salt and pepper. Repeat layers and seasoning. Cover and cook about 20 minutes or until vegetables and potatoes are tender, stirring and turning frequently. Sprinkle with thyme and cool slightly. Meanwhile, in a large bowl, whisk eggs with salt and pepper to taste. Add potato mixture to eggs. Wipe skillet clean. Heat remaining 1 tablespoon oil in the clean skillet over medium heat. Pour egg and potato mixture into skillet; sprinkle with Parmesan cheese. Cover and cook until eggs are just set, about 10 minutes. Slide onto serving platter. Sprinkle parsley and capers over top and cut into wedges to serve. *Serves 4.*

Pasta with Meatballs

Sauce

2 cans (6 ounces each) tomato paste
3 cups water
1 teaspoon basil
1 teaspoon oregano
1 bay leaf
1 clove garlic, minced
1 medium onion, chopped
1 tablespoon salt
Dash of pepper
2 or 3 links Italian sausage (optional), cooked
    and coarsely chopped

Meatballs

½ pound lean ground beef
½ cup fine, dry bread crumbs or cracker
    crumbs
1 egg
1 small onion, finely chopped
1 clove garlic, minced
2 tablespoons grated Romano or Parmesan
    cheese
Pinch of oregano
Pinch of basil
Salt and pepper to taste

Other ingredients

8 ounces uncooked mostaccioli or rigatoni
    pasta
2 hard-boiled eggs, sliced
½ cup grated mozzarella cheese
Grated Romano or Parmesan cheese

To make sauce: In a large kettle, combine tomato paste, water, basil, oregano, bay leaf, garlic, onion, salt, pepper, and sausage, if desired. Cover and simmer over low heat for 2 hours, stirring occasionally. If sauce becomes too thick and begins to stick to the sides of the kettle, add a little water. About 15 minutes before serving, remove the lid so that the sauce can thicken. Sauce should be heavy and smooth. While sauce is cooking, prepare the meatballs and pasta.

To make meatballs: In a large bowl, combine ground beef, crumbs, egg, onion, garlic, cheese, oregano, basil, salt, and pepper. Mix well. Roll into meatballs, about ¾-inch in diameter; place in a single layer in a shallow baking dish. Bake at 350 degrees F. for about 10 minutes. (Note: meatballs may also be browned in oil in a large frying pan.)

Cook pasta according to directions on package and drain. Layer ingredients in the following order in an 8-inch-square baking dish: a small amount of sauce on the bottom; then pasta, meatballs, and egg slices; then another layer of sauce; then the mozzarella cheese. Reserve about 1 cup sauce to pour over individual servings after baking. Sprinkle with Romano or Parmesan cheese and bake, uncovered, at 350 degrees F. for 20 minutes or until heated through. Remove from the oven and let cool slightly before cutting into squares for serving. Pour remaining sauce over individual servings. *Serves 4.*

Fettuccine Roma

½ cup butter
1 to 2 cups cubed ham
1 cup sliced mushrooms (optional)
1 cup light cream
12 ounces fettuccine pasta, cooked according
    to directions on package
1 cup grated Parmesan cheese
Salt and pepper to taste

Melt butter in a heavy skillet or large baking dish. Add ham and mushrooms, if desired, and stir-fry until mushrooms are soft. Add cream and heat through. Stir in cooked fettuccine and cheese. Sprinkle with salt and pepper. Toss gently until pasta is well coated with cheese. *Serves 6.*

2½ cups flour
½ teaspoon salt
¼ cup butter
¼ cup shortening
1 egg, lightly beaten
¼ cup water (approximately)
Choice of fillings (recipes follow)

Stir flour and salt together in a medium bowl. Cut in butter and shortening with a pastry blender until mixture is crumbly. Add egg and enough water to make a soft dough. Roll dough out to ⅛-inch thickness on a lightly floured surface. Cut 8-inch circles (use the lid from a small saucepan as a guide, if desired) and place them on a lightly greased cookie sheet. Place ⅓ to ½ cup of desired filling in the center of each circle. Fold dough in half over filling, moisten edges with water, and press edges firmly together with a fork. Bake at 400 degrees F. for 25 minutes. *Makes 14.*

Beef Filling

1 tablespoon vegetable oil
3 onions, chopped
½ pound lean ground beef
½ teaspoon paprika
½ teaspoon cumin
½ teaspoon salt
¼ teaspoon pepper
10 green olives, sliced
¼ cup raisins
2 hard-boiled eggs

Heat oil in a medium frying pan. Add onions and sauté until clear. Add ground beef and cook until well browned and crumbly. Stir in paprika, cumin, salt, and pepper. Cook over low heat, stirring frequently, for 15 to 20 minutes to blend flavors. Remove from heat, add olives and raisins, and stir well. Slice eggs the long way into 7 slices each. On each circle of dough, place ⅓ to ½ cup of filling and top with a slice of egg. Seal and cook as directed.

Spiced Beef Filling

2 tablespoons vegetable oil
1 pound lean, boneless beef, cooked and
    shredded
1 onion, diced
1 clove garlic, minced
2 tomatoes, chopped
1 apple, peeled, cored, and chopped
¼ cup raisins, plumped in hot water and
    drained
⅛ teaspoon cinnamon
Pinch of cloves
Pinch of cumin
½ cup beef broth or water
Salt to taste

Heat oil in a medium frying pan. Add beef, onion, and garlic and cook until onion is tender. Stir in tomatoes, apple, raisins, cinnamon, cloves, cumin, and broth or water. Simmer until liquid is absorbed, about 25 minutes. Add salt to taste. Spoon onto dough circles, seal, and cook as directed.

Chicken Filling

4 cups diced cooked chicken
2 packages (8 ounces each) cream cheese with
    chives
4 tablespoons minced fresh parsley

Mix chicken, cream cheese, and parsley together in a medium bowl. Spoon onto dough circles, seal, and cook as directed.

Ham and Cheese Filling

4 cups finely chopped ham
1⅓ cups grated Swiss cheese
¼ cup chopped fresh tomatoes
2 tablespoons hot pepper sauce or
    Worcestershire sauce

Mix ham, cheese, tomatoes, and hot pepper or Worcestershire sauce together in a medium bowl. Spoon onto dough circles, seal, and cook as directed.

Apple Filling

4 cups chopped apples
¼ cup sugar
4 teaspoons cinnamon

Stir apples together with sugar and cinnamon in a small bowl. Spoon onto dough circles, seal, and cook as directed.

Quiche Lorraine
France

1 pastry shell, partially baked
¾ cup finely chopped ham
1 cup grated Swiss cheese
6 slices bacon, cooked and crumbled
3 eggs
1 cup heavy cream
Salt and pepper to taste
Nutmeg to taste

Preheat oven to 375 degrees F. Sprinkle ham pieces in the bottom of the pastry shell. Layer Swiss cheese and bacon over ham. Beat eggs with cream and add salt, pepper, and nutmeg. Pour over ingredients in pie crust. Bake in preheated oven for 30 to 40 minutes or until set. *Serves 6.*

Chili Verde
Mexico

2 pounds boneless pork
2 tablespoons vegetable oil
2 large yellow onions, chopped
4 cloves garlic, minced
Salt and pepper to taste
2 cups water
4 raw Anaheim green chilies, chopped
2 tablespoons butter
2 tablespoons flour
2 cans (4 ounces) Anaheim green chilies
8 bean or cheese burritos

Cut pork into cubes. Heat oil in large frying pan; add pork cubes and cook over medium heat, stirring frequently, until browned. Add chopped onions and garlic and continue cooking, stirring occasionally, until onions are tender. Sprinkle with salt and pepper to taste. Add 2 cups water, cover, and simmer for 20 minutes. Add chopped raw green chilies and additional water if needed. Let simmer, covered, until meat is tender when tested with a fork.

Melt butter in a small frying pan. Stir in flour and cook over medium heat, stirring constantly, until mixture is a medium brown color. Set aside. When meat is tender, add the butter-flour mixture and continue cooking, stirring well, until thickened. Add canned green chilies and let simmer for about 10 minutes. Serve over bean or cheese burritos. *Serves 8.*

Chicken and Prosciutto Cannelloni *Italy*

Filling

1 pound boneless, skinless chicken breasts
6 ounces prosciutto or ham, thinly sliced
2 tablespoons butter or margarine
1 large onion, chopped
2 egg yolks
⅔ cup Parmesan cheese
1 cup ricotta cheese
¼ teaspoon nutmeg
Salt and white pepper to taste

Sauce

3 tablespoons vegetable oil
2 medium onions, finely chopped
2 cloves garlic, minced or pressed
1 can (28 ounces) Italian-style tomatoes with liquid
1 can (16 ounces) Italian-style tomatoes with liquid
1½ tablespoons dried mint leaves
1½ teaspoons dried basil leaves
1 cup chicken broth
½ cup whipping cream
Salt and pepper to taste

Other ingredients

12 egg-roll skins
1 pound teleme or Monterey Jack cheese

To make filling: Cut chicken into ½-inch pieces. Set aside. Coarsely chop prosciutto or ham. Set aside. Melt butter or margarine in a large frying pan over medium heat. Add the onion and sauté until tender. Add chicken and continue cooking, stirring frequently, until meat is no longer pink. Remove from heat; add prosciutto. Whirl mixture in a food processor (or mince with a knife) until coarsely ground. Place in a bowl and add egg yolks, Parmesan and ricotta cheeses, and nutmeg. Season to taste with salt and white pepper. Set aside.

To make sauce: Heat oil in a large frying pan over medium heat. Add onions and garlic and sauté until tender. Add the two cans of tomatoes with liquid, mint, basil, and chicken broth. Break up the tomatoes with a spoon. Simmer, uncovered, until sauce is slightly thickened and reduced to 6 cups (about 20 minutes). Stir in whipping cream. Add salt and pepper to taste.

To make cannelloni: Mound about ⅓ cup filling along one long edge of each egg-roll skin; roll to close. Spread half of the sauce evenly in the bottom of a 13 x 9-inch glass baking dish. Place the cannelloni in the dish, seam side down and slightly apart. Spread with remaining sauce. Cut cheese into 12 slices, each slightly larger than top of each cannelloni. Place one slice on each cannelloni. Bake, uncovered, at 400 degrees F. for 30 to 40 minutes or until heated through. *Serves 6.*

Summer Spaghetti *Italy*

6 very ripe tomatoes
Boiling water
1 package (16 ounces) spaghetti noodles
2 tablespoons butter
1 teaspoon salt
1 teaspoon basil
½ teaspoon pepper
¼ cup lemon juice
2 tablespoons fresh snipped parsley
2 cloves garlic, minced
3 tablespoons olive oil

Dip tomatoes in boiling water for 15 seconds. Peel off skins while hot. Dice tomatoes, put them in a strainer, and place them over a bowl to drain. Allow to cool about 1 hour.

Fill a large saucepan with water and bring to a boil. Add noodles and cook until just tender. Drain noodles in a large colander and return to saucepan. Top with butter. Add salt, basil, pepper, lemon juice, parsley, garlic, and olive oil; blend well. Toss in tomatoes. Serve immediately. *Serves 8.*

Seashells with Cottage Cheese

Poland

½ cup butter or margarine
1 large onion, diced
1 tablespoon diced green bell pepper
1 package (16 ounces) small seashell
    macaroni, cooked and drained
Salt and pepper to taste
1 pint cottage cheese

Melt butter or margarine in a large frying pan; add onion and bell pepper and sauté until tender. Add macaroni and salt and pepper to taste. Mix in cottage cheese and heat through. Serve immediately. *Serves 4.*

Linguini with Red Clam Sauce

Italy

2 cans (6½ ounces each) minced clams
2 tablespoons olive oil
½ cup chopped onion
1 clove garlic, minced
1 tablespoon snipped fresh parsley
1 can (14 ounces) tomato sauce
1 can (6 ounces) tomato paste
1 teaspoon crushed dried basil leaves
½ teaspoon sugar
⅛ teaspoon pepper
1½ cups water
1 package (16 ounces) linguini pasta
Grated Parmesan cheese

Drain clams, reserving liquid. Heat oil in a large frying pan; add onion, garlic, and parsley and sauté until onion is tender. Stir in tomato sauce, tomato paste, reserved clam liquid, basil, sugar, pepper, and water. Stir until well blended, cover, and simmer 1 hour.

Cook linguini according to package directions. Drain well. Place linguini on a large serving dish. Add clams to sauce and heat through. Pour sauce over linguini and sprinkle with Parmesan cheese. *Serves 6.*

Rice and Baby Shrimp

Tahiti

1 teaspoon olive oil
1 cup uncooked converted rice
1 large onion, minced
1 clove garlic, pressed
1 teaspoon salt
1 teaspoon cumin
½ teaspoon turmeric
¼ teaspoon red pepper
¼ teaspoon cloves
2 cans (14 ounces each) chicken broth
½ teaspoon coconut extract
1 pound cooked baby shrimp
1 cup raisins
1 cup frozen peas, thawed
1 red bell pepper, diced
½ cup unsweetened flaked coconut (optional)

Heat oil in a large frying pan over medium heat; add rice, onion, and garlic and sauté until rice is browned. Stir in salt, cumin, turmeric, red pepper, and cloves. Add chicken broth and coconut extract. Reduce heat, cover, and simmer for 20 minutes. Add shrimp, raisins, peas, and bell pepper; stir until well mixed and heated through. Sprinkle with coconut, if desired. *Serves 6.*

Pictured on page 66

Spinach Pie (Torta Pascualina)   *Uruguay*

Filling

1 medium onion, chopped
1 clove garlic, minced
4 tablespoons olive oil
4 bunches fresh spinach, washed and
    chopped, or 6 packages (8 ounces each)
    frozen chopped spinach
Salt and pepper to taste
¼ teaspoon oregano
1 bay leaf, crushed
1 cup grated Parmesan cheese
2 eggs
½ pound mushrooms, chopped (optional)

Dough

2 cups flour
¼ cup light butter
½ cup water
1 teaspoon salt
5 hard-boiled eggs
1 egg yolk, beaten

To make filling: Sauté onion and garlic in olive oil. Add spinach. Cook about 5 minutes. Add salt and pepper to taste. Add oregano and crushed bay leaf. Remove from heat and drain. Add Parmesan cheese, eggs, and mushrooms, if desired.

To make dough: In a medium bowl, mix together flour, butter, water, and salt to make a soft dough. Add more water, if needed. Divide in half. Spray a 9-inch springform pan or a 9-inch pie tin with nonstick cooking spray. Roll half of the dough out to fit pan. Top with spinach mixture. Slice the hard-boiled eggs very thin and lay them over the filling. Roll out remaining half of dough and place over top; flute edge. Brush with egg yolk. Bake at 400 degrees F. for 45 minutes or until golden. *Serves 8.*

VEGETABLES AND SIDE DISHES

Potatoes with Cheese
Colombia

12 small red potatoes (each 1½ to 2 inches in diameter), scrubbed clean
2 tablespoons butter or margarine
1 medium onion, finely chopped
4 green onions, cut into 1-inch lengths
2 large tomatoes, peeled, seeded, and chopped
½ cup whipping cream
1 tablespoon finely chopped fresh cilantro
½ teaspoon crushed dried oregano leaves
¼ teaspoon cumin
Salt and pepper to taste
1 cup shredded mozzarella cheese

Put potatoes in a large saucepan and add water to a depth of 2 inches. Bring to a boil over high heat. Cover, reduce heat, and simmer about 20 minutes or until potatoes are tender when pierced with a fork. Melt butter or margarine in a large frying pan over medium heat. Add chopped onion and green onions and sauté until tender. Add tomatoes and cook, stirring occasionally, for 5 minutes. Add cream, cilantro, oregano, and cumin; then season to taste with salt and pepper. Slowly add cheese, stirring constantly until cheese is completely melted. Drain potatoes and place in a serving dish; spoon sauce over top. *Serves 6.*

Potato Pie
Peru

3 tablespoons vegetable oil
1 large onion, chopped fine
1 clove garlic, minced
¾ cup grated fresh tomatoes
3 large potatoes, cooked, peeled, and sliced
8 ounces cheddar cheese, sliced thin
2 egg whites
Pinch of salt
2 egg yolks
2 tablespoons cream
⅛ teaspoon salt

Heat oil in a large frying pan. Add onion and garlic; sauté until tender. Add tomatoes and simmer over low heat for 8 minutes. Grease the bottom and sides of an 8-inch square baking dish. Cover the bottom of the dish with half of the potatoes. Spoon half of tomato sauce over potatoes and place half of the cheese slices on sauce. Repeat procedure with remaining ingredients. Beat egg whites until foamy. Add pinch of salt. In a small dish, mix egg yolks, cream, and ⅛ teaspoon salt. Fold in egg whites and spoon over last cheese layer. Bake at 350 degrees F. until golden brown, about 1 hour. *Serves 4.*

Straw and Hay
Italy

4 ounces thin spinach noodles
4 ounces fettuccine noodles
3 tablespoons butter
1 clove garlic, minced
½ cup frozen petite peas, thawed
¼ pound fresh mushrooms, sliced
¾ cup whipping cream
½ teaspoon salt
Pepper to taste
¼ cup grated Parmesan cheese

Cook noodles in salted water according to directions on package until they are tender but firm. Drain and toss with 1½ tablespoons butter. Cover and set aside. In a large saucepan, melt remaining 1½ tablespoons butter. Add garlic and sauté until golden. Spoon out garlic and discard. In the same butter, sauté peas and mushrooms over low heat for 5 minutes. At the same time, heat cream in a small pan. (Do not boil.) With the frying pan still over the heat, add noodles, cream, salt, and pepper to the vegetables, tossing vigorously with a long-handled spoon and fork. Remove from heat and quickly stir in cheese. Serve immediately. *Serves 4.*

Potato Pancakes *Czech Republic*

2 tablespoons lemon juice
4 cups water
2 cups grated uncooked potatoes
2 tablespoons flour
2 eggs, well beaten
1 tablespoon finely chopped onion
1 teaspoon salt
1 teaspoon sugar
2 tablespoons chopped parsley (optional)
1 teaspoon caraway seeds (optional)
2 to 3 tablespoons butter or margarine
Sour cream (optional)
Sugar (optional)

In a large bowl, combine lemon juice and water. Add grated potatoes; stir well, then pour mixture through a colander. Squeeze as much liquid out of potatoes as possible and spread out on paper towels to drain further. In a medium bowl, mix flour, eggs, onion, salt, sugar, parsley (if desired), caraway (if desired), and potatoes. Beat well. Melt 1 or 2 tablespoons butter or margarine on a hot griddle. Place a scant 2 tablespoons potato mixture on hot griddle and spread very thin. Fry on both sides. Repeat with remaining potato mixture, adding more butter or margarine to griddle as needed. Serve plain, dot with sour cream, or sprinkle with sugar. Keep warm in a 200 degree F. oven until ready to serve. *Makes 24.*

Lemon Carrots *Israel*

3 cups peeled, sliced carrots
½ teaspoon salt
Boiling water
1 teaspoon dried parsley flakes
½ teaspoon sugar
½ teaspoon paprika
1 tablespoon butter
Juice of ½ lemon

In a large saucepan, simmer carrots in salted water until tender but not pulpy. Drain, add remaining ingredients, and heat through, shaking pan so carrots will be well coated. *Serves 6.*

Green Beans and Corn *Germany*

3 slices bacon, cut in small pieces
1 small onion, chopped
1 can (16 ounces) green beans
1 tablespoon sugar
¼ cup vinegar
1 can (12 ounces) whole kernel corn, drained
Salt and pepper to taste

Brown bacon with onion in a large frying pan. Drain liquid from beans into pan; cook down to about ⅓ cup. Stir in sugar and vinegar. Add beans and corn. Season to taste with salt and pepper; heat through. *Serves 6.*

Orzo with Browned Butter Sauce *Greece*

8 ounces uncooked orzo pasta
⅓ cup butter
3 tablespoons grated Parmesan cheese

Cook pasta according to directions on package. Drain in a colander and set aside. In a small saucepan, melt butter over medium-high heat; cook, stirring constantly, until butter turns brown. Place hot, drained pasta in a serving bowl; pour butter and Parmesan cheese over pasta and stir to combine. Serve immediately. *Serves 4.*

Glazed Onions

Belgium

¼ cup sugar
3 tablespoons water
3 tablespoons butter or margarine
1 tablespoon white wine vinegar
1 tablespoon tomato paste
½ teaspoon salt
½ teaspoon crushed dried thyme leaves
⅛ teaspoon pepper
1 bay leaf
2 packages (16 ounces each) frozen small
    white onions
¾ cup raisins

Combine sugar, water, butter or margarine, vinegar, tomato paste, salt, thyme, pepper, and bay leaf in a large frying pan. Bring mixture to a boil, stirring to dissolve sugar. Add onions and raisins. Return to boiling. Reduce heat, cover, and simmer 10 minutes. Uncover and cook 20 to 25 minutes longer over medium heat, stirring frequently, until onions appear glazed. Discard bay leaf. Serve warm. *Serves 8.*

Fried Potatoes

Hungary

1 onion, finely chopped
2 tablespoons rendered bacon fat
4 medium potatoes, sliced
2 teaspoons paprika
Salt to taste
½ cup water
Dash of pepper

In a large frying pan, brown onion in the bacon fat. Add potatoes, 1 teaspoon of the paprika, and salt. Cover tightly; cook over medium heat for 10 minutes, stirring occasionally. Reduce heat, add water, pepper, and remaining paprika. Cover and cook for 10 minutes longer or until potatoes are tender. *Serves 4.*

Beans Granados

Chile

½ pound dry red kidney beans
5 cups water
4 cups water
1 teaspoon salt
2 tablespoons butter or margarine
1 cup chopped onion
2 cloves garlic, minced
1½ cups fresh corn kernels, cut from cob
    (about 3 ears)
1 cup acorn squash or other winter squash,
    cut in ½-inch cubes
¾ cup condensed beef broth

Combine beans in a large kettle with the 5 cups water. Bring to a boil. Reduce heat and simmer, uncovered, for 2 minutes. Cover and let stand at room temperature for 1 hour. Drain the beans in a colander. Return beans to kettle with 4 cups fresh water and salt, and bring to a boil. Reduce heat, cover, and cook 1 to 1½ hours or until beans are tender. Drain. Melt butter or margarine in a large frying pan; add onion and garlic and sauté until tender. Add the cooked beans, corn, squash, and beef broth. Cover and cook until vegetables are tender (about 10 minutes). *Serves 4.*

Broccoli Parmesan
Italy

4 packages (10 ounces each) frozen chopped
    broccoli
¼ cup shortening
½ pound fresh mushrooms, sliced, or 1 can
    (8 ounces) sliced mushrooms
1 clove garlic, minced
1 can (6 ounces) tomato paste
¼ cup flour
1 teaspoon salt
¼ teaspoon nutmeg
Pepper to taste
¼ cup grated Parmesan cheese

Cook broccoli according to directions on package. Drain, reserving 1 to 1½ cups liquid. Melt shortening in a large frying pan; add mushrooms and garlic and sauté briefly. Stir in tomato paste, flour, reserved broccoli liquid, salt, nutmeg, and pepper. Simmer, uncovered, for 15 minutes. Arrange broccoli in an 11 x 7-inch baking dish. Cover with sauce; sprinkle with cheese. Bake at 350 degrees F. for 30 minutes. *Serves 12.*

Marinated Tomato Slices
Italy

Pictured on page 83

3 large tomatoes, sliced
Olive oil
1 teaspoon basil
1 teaspoon rosemary
1 teaspoon oregano
½ teaspoon salt
¼ teaspoon freshly ground pepper

Place tomatoes in large bowl; cover with olive oil. Combine basil, rosemary, oregano, salt, and pepper; sprinkle over tomatoes and toss to blend well. Cover and refrigerate for several hours. Drain tomatoes, reserving marinade if desired for future use with meat or other vegetables. Serve tomatoes cold. *Serves 6.*

Stuffed Zucchini
Italy

6 medium zucchini
1 teaspoon salt
2 eggs, well beaten
1½ cups grated sharp cheddar cheese
½ cup small-curd cottage cheese
2 tablespoons minced fresh parsley
½ teaspoon salt
½ teaspoon pepper

Preheat oven to 350 degrees F. Cut ends from zucchini and place zucchini in a large saucepan. Cover with water; stir in 1 teaspoon salt. Bring to a boil and cook for about 12 minutes or until tender but still firm. Drain. Halve lengthwise; scoop out centers, leaving shells. Invert shells on paper towels to drain. Mix eggs, cheeses, parsley, ½ teaspoon salt, and pepper. Fill zucchini shells with mixture. Arrange in greased baking dish. Bake uncovered in preheated oven for 15 minutes. Serve hot or cold. *Serves 6.*

Zucchini Crisps
Greece

⅓ cup flour
¼ teaspoon salt
⅛ teaspoon pepper
1 egg, slightly beaten
½ cup cold water
1 cup olive oil
6 small zucchini, trimmed and thinly sliced

Combine flour, salt, pepper, egg, and water; blend well. Heat oil in a large frying pan. Dip zucchini into batter, allowing excess batter to drip off. Fry in hot oil until golden brown on each side. Drain; serve at once. *Serves 6.*

Spinach in Einbrenner Sauce
Germany

1 package (10 ounces) frozen chopped
   spinach
1 cup water
1 beef bouillon cube
2 tablespoons butter or margarine
1 small onion, finely chopped
1 tablespoon flour
Salt and pepper to taste

In a medium saucepan, cook spinach in 1 cup water with bouillon cube until done. Drain, reserving liquid. Set spinach aside. Melt butter or margarine in a medium frying pan; add onion and sauté until tender. Stir in flour. Add reserved spinach liquid slowly, stirring constantly, until mixture is consistency of gravy. Add spinach and mix well. Heat through and add salt and pepper to taste. *Serves 4.*

Eggplant Parmigiana
Italy

1 tablespoon butter
½ cup chopped onion
2 cloves garlic, minced
1 can (14 ounces) diced tomatoes with liquid
⅓ cup tomato paste
2 tablespoons snipped fresh parsley
2 teaspoons crushed dried basil leaves
½ teaspoon crushed dried thyme leaves
¼ teaspoon salt
¼ teaspoon pepper
2 medium eggplants, peeled and cut crosswise
   into ½-inch slices
Salt
2 tablespoons vegetable oil
½ cup Parmesan cheese
6 ounces mozzarella cheese, thinly sliced

Melt butter in a large frying pan; add onion and garlic and cook until tender. Add tomatoes with liquid, tomato paste, parsley, basil, thyme, salt, and pepper; stir well. Bring to a boil. Reduce heat and simmer, uncovered, about 15 minutes or until mixture is slightly thickened. You should have about 2½ cups of mixture.

Sprinkle eggplant slices lightly with salt and let drain for 30 minutes. Pat dry with paper towels. Heat oil in a large frying pan; add eggplant slices and fry until golden brown. Preheat oven to 400 degrees F. Spread about ½ cup tomato sauce mixture in the bottom of an 8 x 12-inch glass baking dish. Arrange a single layer of eggplant over the sauce, cutting slices to fit. Top with half the remaining sauce and half the Parmesan and mozzarella cheeses. Repeat layers. Bake, uncovered, for 20 minutes or until heated through. *Serves 10.*

Spaetzle
Germany

2 cups flour
1 teaspoon salt
2 eggs
¾ cup milk
5 quarts water
½ teaspoon salt
¼ cup melted butter
½ cup toasted buttered bread crumbs
   (optional)

Combine flour and 1 teaspoon salt in a mixing bowl. Mix eggs and milk together and add to the flour mixture. Mix well for 2 or 3 minutes and let rest for 15 minutes. In a large kettle, bring water to a boil; add ½ teaspoon salt. Place batter in a coarse-sieved deep-fat fryer basket or colander with ¼-inch holes. Hold over pan of boiling salted water. Press the batter through the holes with the back of a wooden spoon or rubber spatula. If the dough is too thick to push through, thin it with a little milk. Boil for 6 to 8 minutes or until tender. Remove with a slotted spoon and drain in a colander. When all spaetzle are cooked, rinse with cold water and drain well. Put in bowl and mix in melted butter. Turn mixture into an 8-inch square baking dish and bake, uncovered, at 300 degrees F. for 20 to 30 minutes. Just before serving, top with toasted crumbs, if desired. *Serves 4.*

Sweet and Sour Red Cabbage — *Germany*

1 medium red cabbage, cored and thinly
   sliced
⅓ cup salt
Water
4 pieces bacon, cut into ½-inch pieces
5 tablespoons brown sugar
¼ cup white vinegar
2 small apples, cut in quarters

Put cabbage into a large pan and sprinkle with the salt. Knead salt into cabbage with hands until cabbage is limp, about 8 to 10 minutes. Cover with cool water and let sit. In a large frying pan, cook bacon until crumbly; drain the grease off. Lift cabbage out of water with hands and rinse in running water, letting water run through fingers. Then put cabbage into a colander and run water over it. Let drain. Put drained cabbage into saucepan with bacon; add brown sugar, vinegar, and apples. Do not add any water. Cover and simmer on low heat for 1½ hours, stirring occasionally. *Serves 6.*

Cheesy Cauliflower — *England*

1 medium head cauliflower
1 cup water
3 tablespoons butter
3 tablespoons flour
¼ teaspoon dry mustard
¼ teaspoon salt
1 cup milk
½ cup grated sharp cheddar cheese

Remove outer leaves and stalks of cauliflower. Break into florets. Place in medium saucepan with water and steam 5 to 7 minutes or until tender. Melt butter over low heat in heavy saucepan. Blend in flour, mustard, and salt. Slowly stir in milk and cook, stirring constantly, until thick. Add grated cheese and stir until melted. Place cauliflower in serving dish and pour cheese sauce over top. *Serves 6.*

Potatoes and Cabbage — *England*

6 medium potatoes, peeled and quartered
Water
2 teaspoons salt
2½ to 3 cups shredded cabbage
1 cup chopped onion
Boiling salted water
¼ cup butter or margarine
½ to ¾ cup milk
1 teaspoon salt
⅛ teaspoon pepper
1 tablespoon snipped fresh parsley

Place potatoes in a large saucepan; cover with water and add 2 teaspoons salt. Boil until potatoes are tender, about 20 minutes. Drain. Meanwhile, in a medium saucepan, cook cabbage and onion together in a small amount of boiling salted water for 15 minutes. Drain. Mash potatoes, using electric mixer. Beat in butter or margarine and as much milk as necessary to make a fluffy mixture. Add 1 teaspoon salt and pepper. Stir in cabbage and onion. Top with parsley. *Serves 6.*

Marinated Tomato Slices (page 80)

Traditional English Dressing
England

6 cans (14 ounces each) beef broth
4 cups uncooked long-grain rice
4 cups water
2 large onions, chopped
2 cups chopped celery
1 large green bell pepper, chopped
1 large red bell pepper, chopped
Cold water
1 pound sweet Italian sausage
1 pound lean ground beef
1 tablespoon pepper
1 tablespoon savory
2 teaspoons salt
2 teaspoons dry mustard
2 teaspoons marjoram
2 teaspoons sage
1 teaspoon oregano

In a large saucepan, bring broth to a full boil; add rice. Reduce heat, cover, and simmer for 20 minutes. In another large saucepan, bring 4 cups water to a boil and add onions, celery, and green and red peppers. Boil until almost tender. Drain and cover vegetables with cold water. Set aside.

In a large frying pan, brown the sausage and ground beef until crumbly, making sure the sausage is cooked through. Drain and set aside.

In an extra-large mixing bowl, combine rice, onions, celery, and peppers. Add the meat mixture, pepper, savory, salt, mustard, marjoram, sage, and oregano. Mix thoroughly. Turn entire mixture into large greased baking dish or dishes. Cover with foil and bake at 350 degrees F. for 45 to 60 minutes. *Serves 15.*

Egg Foo Yong
China

3 cups mung bean sprouts
1 chicken thigh, cooked
¾ cup tiny boiled shrimp (optional)
10 fresh mushrooms, thinly sliced
1 red or green bell pepper, thinly sliced
4 or 5 eggs
Soy sauce

Rinse bean sprouts in a colander. Set aside to drain. Dice chicken meat and shrimp, if desired. Shake sprouts and crunch them 15 times with both hands. In a large bowl, toss together sprouts, mushrooms, bell pepper, chicken, and shrimp. Preheat a large griddle. Whip eggs in a small bowl until light yellow. Pour into vegetable-chicken mixture and mix until everything is well coated with egg mixture. Drop batter by large scoops onto hot griddle and fry like pancakes. Flip when browned. Sprinkle with soy sauce. *Serves 6.*

Garden Rice
Chile

1 teaspoon vegetable oil
2 cups uncooked rice
3 cups diced potatoes
2 carrots, diced
1 onion, diced
4 or 5 cups hot water
3 or 4 cubes chicken bouillon
¼ teaspoon cumin
¼ teaspoon paprika
1 bay leaf
Salt and pepper to taste
½ cup peas

In a large saucepan, combine the oil, rice, potatoes, carrots, and onion; stir-fry for 3 to 5 minutes. Add 4 cups hot water, 3 cubes bouillon, cumin, paprika, bay leaf, salt, and pepper. Cover and cook for 15 minutes, stirring occasionally. Add the peas. If rice is not tender and vegetables not yet cooked through, add an additional 1 cup water with 1 bouillon cube. Cover and continue cooking until water is absorbed and rice is tender. Discard bay leaf. *Serves 6.*

Clockwise from top: Chocolate-Dipped Orange Cookies (page 92), Crescent Cookies (page 91), Black-and-White Biscotti (page 95), Raspberry Sticks (page 88)

Fried Rice

Thailand

3 tablespoons butter
2 teaspoons minced fresh gingerroot or
    crystallized ginger
1 clove garlic, minced
½ cup thinly sliced pork
6 shrimp, shelled, deveined, and chopped
½ cup chopped scallions or green onions
5 to 6 cups cooked rice
Salt and pepper to taste
2 eggs
Chopped cucumbers
Chopped fresh tomatoes
Chopped scallions

Melt butter in a large frying pan. Add ginger and garlic; sauté for 2 minutes. Add pork and sauté until tender. Add shrimp and sauté until the shrimp turns pink. Stir in scallions or green onions. Add rice and stir-fry until rice is heated through. Add salt and pepper to taste. Crack eggs over rice and stir-fry until eggs are cooked. Serve garnished with chopped cucumbers, tomatoes, and scallions. *Serves 6.*

Hot Pepper Sauce (Pebre)

Chile

3 large tomatoes, peeled, diced, and smashed
1 onion, finely diced
3 cloves garlic, diced
3 or 4 sprigs fresh parsley, chopped
1 teaspoon vegetable oil
1 teaspoon vinegar
Fresh ground chili paste to taste (may be
    found at an Oriental market)
Salt to taste

In a medium bowl, combine tomatoes, onion, garlic, parsley, oil, vinegar, chili paste, and salt. Mix well. Refrigerate until ready to serve. Serve with meats, barbecue, potatoes, or any other dish you wish to spice up. *Makes 1 cup (16 servings of 1 tablespoon each).*

COOKIES

Filled Cookies

Argentina

Filling

1 can (14 ounces) sweetened condensed milk
Boiling water
1 tablespoon melted butter or margarine
2 tablespoons lemon extract

Cookies

½ cup flour
1 teaspoon baking powder
1¼ cups cornstarch
6 tablespoons butter
¾ cup sugar
Grated peel from ½ lemon
1 egg
1 egg yolk

Topping

1 cup sweetened, shredded coconut

To make filling: Fill a saucepan with enough water to cover the unopened can of condensed milk and bring water to a boil. Submerge unopened can of condensed milk in water, reduce heat, and simmer for 3 hours. Add hot water as needed to keep can covered. Remove can of milk from pan and let cool. Open can and put caramelized milk in a medium bowl with melted butter or margarine and lemon extract. Beat until smooth. Refrigerate until ready to use.

To make cookies: Preheat oven to 350 degrees F. Sift together the flour, baking powder, and cornstarch. In a small mixer bowl, cream together butter and sugar until smooth. Add grated lemon peel, egg, and egg yolk and continue beating. Add flour mixture a little at a time and mix until dough is smooth. Put dough on a lightly floured surface and roll out to ⅛-inch thickness. Cut into 2-inch circles, using a cookie cutter or the rim of a glass. Arrange circles on a lightly greased baking sheet and bake for 15 minutes or until lightly browned. Allow cookies to cool for 1 minute before removing from baking sheet. Cool completely on wire rack. When cool, spread 1 teaspoon filling on each cookie and sprinkle with coconut. *Makes 3 dozen.*

Spice Cookies (Spekulatius)

Germany

4 cups flour
2 teaspoons baking powder
1¼ cups sugar
½ teaspoon cloves
1 teaspoon cinnamon
2 eggs
1 teaspoon milk
1 cup butter or margarine

Preheat oven to 350 degrees F. Sift flour, baking powder, sugar, cloves, and cinnamon together into a large bowl. Add eggs and milk and knead thoroughly. Cut butter or margarine into pieces and knead into the mixture. Knead thoroughly until you have a smooth dough. Roll out ⅛-inch thick and cut out cookies with your favorite cookie cutters. Place on greased baking sheet and bake about 12 to 15 minutes or until brown. Note: These cookies are best if made 3 weeks before using. Store in airtight container. *Makes 3 dozen.*

Pictured on page 84

Raspberry Sticks

Finland

1 cup butter
¾ cup sugar
1 egg
1 teaspoon vanilla
2½ cups flour
¼ teaspoon salt
1 to 2 tablespoons water (if needed)
Raspberry jam

In a large mixer bowl, cream butter and sugar together until light and fluffy. Add egg and vanilla; beat well. Sift flour and salt together; add to sugar mixture ⅓ at a time, mixing well after each addition. If dough is too stiff, add 1 or 2 tablespoons water. Wrap dough in plastic wrap and chill in refrigerator for about 1 hour.

Preheat oven to 375 degrees F. Cut the chilled dough into 4 pieces. Roll each piece into a rope the length of your cookie sheet. Put ropes onto the cookie sheet, side by side. With your finger, make an indentation all the way down the length of each rope. Bake in preheated oven for 10 minutes. Remove from oven and fill the indentations with raspberry jam. Put back into the oven for another 10 to 12 minutes. Place cookie sheet on rack to cool cookies. Cut on the diagonal. *Makes 3 dozen.*

Citron Cookies

Germany

2 eggs
2 egg yolks
1 cup sugar
2 cups flour
1 cup finely chopped candied citrus peel
Grated peel of 1 lemon
Split blanched almonds
Maraschino cherries

Cream eggs and egg yolks with sugar in a mixing bowl. Beat until smooth and lemon in color. Add flour and mix well. Mix in candied citrus peel and lemon peel. Chill dough in refrigerator for at least 1 hour to make it easier to handle. Work with a small amount of dough at a time. Roll a piece of dough into a strip about 3 inches wide. Cut strip in 2-inch long pieces. Fold each piece in half and place on lightly greased baking sheet. Decorate each with an almond or a cherry. Bake at 350 degrees F. for 15 minutes. Note: These cookies are best if made 2 weeks before using and stored with an apple in an airtight container. *Makes 4 to 5 dozen.*

High Tea Scones

Scotland

Grated peel of 1 lemon
1 tablespoon sugar
½ cup sour cream
¼ teaspoon baking soda
1 egg, beaten
¼ cup vegetable oil
3 tablespoons milk
2 cups flour
3 teaspoons baking powder
1 teaspoon salt
2 tablespoons sugar
½ cup raisins or currants (optional)

Combine lemon peel and 1 tablespoon sugar; set aside. Preheat oven to 425 degrees F. In a small bowl, combine sour cream and baking soda. Add egg, oil, and milk. Set aside. In a large bowl, sift together the flour, baking powder, salt, and 2 tablespoons sugar. Pour the egg mixture into the dry ingredients and stir until flour is just dampened. Stir in raisins or currants, if desired. Place on a floured surface and knead the dough 10 to 15 times. Roll the dough into a circle about ½-inch thick. Sprinkle with the lemon peel mixture. Cut into 12 wedge-shaped pieces and place on a greased baking sheet. Bake in preheated oven for 15 to 20 minutes. *Makes 12.*

Christmas Pinwheels

Finland

Filling

12 ounces pitted prunes
Water
¼ cup sugar
1 tablespoon lemon juice

Dough

2 cups flour
¼ teaspoon baking powder
1 cup butter or margarine, cut in pieces
⅔ cup cold water (approximately)
1 egg, beaten
Powdered sugar

To make filling: Place prunes in a medium saucepan with enough water to cover them; boil gently until soft. Purée in blender and add sugar and lemon juice.

To make dough: Sift together flour and baking powder. Cut in butter or margarine with a pastry blender or fork until mixture resembles small crumbs. Add water gradually and mix just until smooth. Don't overmix. Chill dough 30 minutes. Roll dough into a rectangle on a floured board. Fold into thirds and roll again. Repeat rolling and folding 2 or 3 times for a flaky crust.

Roll dough out into a 12-inch square. Cut into 3-inch squares. Place about 1 tablespoon of filling in the middle of each square. Split each corner from the top to within ½ inch of the center. Fold half of each corner of the square to the center, pinching end together, thus forming a pinwheel. Brush tarts with beaten egg. Bake at 375 degrees F. for 20 minutes. When cool, dust with powdered sugar. *Makes 16.*

Butter Horns

Germany

1½ cups butter, softened
3 cups flour
1 pint small-curd cottage cheese
Apricot, raspberry, or strawberry jam
1 package (3 ounces) cream cheese
1 cup powdered sugar
½ teaspoon vanilla

In a large bowl, blend butter, flour, and cottage cheese with a pastry blender or with your hands just until dough is smooth. Pinch off an amount of dough the size of a golf ball. Roll out on a floured surface into a circle. Cut the circle into fourths. Place a teaspoon of jam in the center of each piece and roll from the large outer end to the pointed tip. Place cookies, tip down, 2 inches apart on a lightly greased baking sheet. Repeat until all the dough is used. Bake at 400 degrees F. until lightly browned, about 8 to 10 minutes.

While cookies are baking, beat cream cheese, powdered sugar, and vanilla together until smooth. Glaze cookies with this mixture while they are still warm. Cool on a wire rack. *Makes 6 dozen.*

Coconut-Cherry Macaroons

France

1 bag (7 ounces) sweetened, shredded coconut, coarsely chopped
½ cup canned soft almond paste
½ cup chopped red candied cherries
½ cup chopped green candied cherries
¼ cup sugar
¼ cup flour
¼ teaspoon salt
2 egg whites, lightly beaten

Preheat oven to 325 degrees F. Line a baking sheet with parchment paper; set aside. In a large bowl, combine coconut, almond paste, candied cherries, sugar, flour, salt, and egg whites. Stir until well mixed. Drop mixture by level tablespoonfuls onto prepared baking sheet, shaping into rounds. Bake in preheated oven for 25 minutes, until lightly browned but still soft in center. Cool on wire rack. *Makes 2 dozen.*

Raspberry Coconut Slice

Australia

Pastry

1 cup flour
1 teaspoon baking powder
¼ cup margarine
2 tablespoons sugar
2 egg yolks, beaten
1½ tablespoons water

Filling

4 tablespoons seedless red raspberry jam

Topping

2⅔ cups sweetened, flaked coconut
¾ cup sugar
1 tablespoon water
4 egg whites
⅛ teaspoon salt
⅓ cup flour

Preheat oven to 350 degrees F. Grease an 11 x 7-inch pan; set aside.

To make pastry: In a medium bowl, sift flour and baking powder. Cut in margarine with a pastry blender or fork until crumbly. Mix in sugar. Combine beaten egg yolks with water and add to flour mixture. Blend until a soft dough forms. Turn pastry onto a lightly floured surface and knead lightly to form a smooth ball of dough. Press dough over the bottom of the prepared pan. Prick well with a fork. Bake in preheated oven for 12 minutes. Cool; then spread jam over baked pastry.

To make topping: In a medium saucepan, combine coconut, sugar, water, 2 of the egg whites, and salt. Stir over medium heat until mix becomes moist and lumpy. Do not allow coconut to become brown. Remove from heat and allow to cool. Sift flour into cooled coconut mixture. In a small bowl, beat remaining 2 egg whites until firm peaks form. Fold into coconut mix; blend well. Spread coconut mixture over top of jam. Bake at 350 degrees F. for 30 to 35 minutes. Cool and slice. *Makes 10 squares.*

Spritz Cookies

Germany

¾ cup butter, softened
¾ cup sugar
1 teaspoon vanilla or almond extract
1½ cups flour
3 egg yolks, beaten
Colored sugar (optional)

Preheat oven to 400 degrees F. Grease a baking sheet and put it into the refrigerator to cool. In a small bowl, cream butter and sugar together until light and fluffy. Add vanilla or almond extract and mix. Stir in the flour alternately with the beaten egg yolks and mix to a soft, pliable dough. Force dough through the large nozzle of a cookie press onto prepared baking sheet, forming circles, knots, or fingers. (If you do not have a cookie press, you may roll dough into small balls and flatten gently with a fork.) Sprinkle with colored sugar, if desired. Bake in preheated oven for 10 minutes. Remove cookies immediately from pan and cool on wire rack. *Makes 3 dozen.*

Shortbread

England

2 cups butter, softened
1 cup sugar
Pinch of salt
4 cups flour
⅓ cup cornstarch

In a large bowl, beat butter, sugar, and salt together until light and fluffy. Mix flour and cornstarch and add to creamed mixture gradually, ½ cup at a time, beating after each addition. Gather dough in a ball and knead on lightly floured surface. With rolling pin, roll out about ½-inch thick. Cut into 2-inch squares and place on ungreased baking sheet. Prick tops with fork. Bake at 375 degrees F. about 15 minutes or until tops are barely brown. Do not overbake. Cool and store in tightly covered container. Shortbread mellows with age and keeps well for a long time. *Makes 5 dozen.*

Macaroons

3 egg whites
⅔ cup plus 1 tablespoon sugar
½ teaspoon vanilla
⅛ teaspoon almond extract
¼ cup flour
⅓ pound chopped hazelnuts or almonds, or
    1⅓ cups sweetened, flaked coconut

Preheat oven to 300 degrees F. In a small bowl, whip egg whites until quite stiff. Gradually mix in sugar, vanilla, and almond extract. Continue to beat until stiff peaks form. Mix flour and nuts or coconut together and fold into egg white mixture. Drop by teaspoonfuls onto greased baking sheet. Bake in preheated oven for 35 minutes. Remove from pan immediately and cool on wire rack. *Makes 3 dozen.*

Ginger Cookies

1 cup shortening
2 cups brown sugar
2 eggs
1 teaspoon vanilla
3½ cups flour
1 teaspoon baking soda
2 teaspoons cream of tartar
2 teaspoons ginger

Preheat oven to 350 degrees F. In a large bowl, cream together shortening and sugar. Add eggs and vanilla; beat until fluffy. Add flour, baking soda, cream of tartar, and ginger. When thoroughly mixed, roll into small balls and place on a greased baking sheet. Flatten with a fork. Bake for 10 minutes. Remove from pan and cool on a wire rack. *Makes 5 dozen.*

Pictured on page 84

Crescent Cookies

1 cup butter
2 egg yolks
2 cups powdered sugar
2¼ cups flour
1 teaspoon cinnamon
½ teaspoon cloves
⅛ teaspoon salt
2 cups ground, blanched almonds
Powdered sugar

Beat butter and egg yolks together in a large bowl. Add powdered sugar and beat until well mixed. Add flour, cinnamon, cloves, salt, and ground almonds. Mix well. Pinch off a piece of dough about the size of a walnut; roll it into a 2-inch rope and form it in a crescent shape. Place on a greased baking sheet. Repeat with remaining dough. Bake at 350 degrees F. for 20 minutes. While cookies are still warm, roll them in powdered sugar. *Makes 2 dozen.*

Oatmeal Cookies

2 cups rolled oats
2 cups flour
1 teaspoon baking powder
1 cup butter
¾ cup sugar
1 egg
½ cup chopped walnuts (optional)
½ cup raisins (optional)

Stir together oats, flour, and baking powder. Add butter, sugar, egg, and walnuts and raisins (if desired). Mix until well blended. Drop by tablespoonfuls onto an ungreased baking sheet. Bake at 350 degrees F. for 10 to 15 minutes or until golden brown. *Makes 3 dozen.*

Sinter Klauss Cookies
Denmark

1 cup butter or margarine
1 cup shortening
1 cup brown sugar
1 cup white sugar
1 teaspoon almond extract
4 cups flour
4 teaspoons cinnamon
1 teaspoon cloves
1 teaspoon allspice
1 teaspoon ginger
½ teaspoon baking soda
½ cup buttermilk or sour milk
½ cup slivered almonds

Preheat oven to 375 degrees F. Cream butter or margarine and shortening with sugars in a large bowl. Add almond extract and mix well. Sift together flour, cinnamon, cloves, allspice, and ginger; set aside. Dissolve baking soda in buttermilk or sour milk and add to creamed mixture alternately with flour mixture. Press dough into a greased 16 x 10-inch jelly-roll pan. Sprinkle nuts on top and bake for 25 to 30 minutes or until light brown. Cool and cut into squares. *Makes 40.*

Pictured on page 84

Chocolate-Dipped Orange Cookies
Mexico

2 cups flour
½ cup yellow cornmeal
1 teaspoon salt
½ teaspoon baking soda
1 cup butter, softened
1 cup sugar
2 egg yolks
1 tablespoon grated orange peel
1 teaspoon orange extract
¼ cup ground walnuts
6 ounces milk chocolate or semi-sweet
    chocolate chips

In a bowl, stir together flour, cornmeal, salt, and baking soda. Set aside. In a large bowl, cream together butter and sugar. Beat in egg yolks, orange peel, and orange extract until fluffy. Add flour mixture and walnuts. Mix well. Divide dough in half. Wrap in plastic and refrigerate for 30 minutes.

Preheat oven to 350 degrees F. Roll half of the dough out to ¼-inch thickness on a lightly floured surface. Cut dough with a floured 3½-inch round or star-shaped cookie cutter. If using round cutter, cut each circle in half. Place 1 inch apart on a lightly greased baking sheet. Repeat with remaining dough. Bake in preheated oven for 10 to 12 minutes or until lightly browned. Cool on a wire rack.

Line a baking sheet with waxed paper. In a small saucepan, melt chocolate over low heat, stirring constantly. (Chocolate may also be melted in microwave; place in a microwave-safe bowl.) Remove from heat. Dip one end of cookies into chocolate; place on prepared sheet. Let stand until chocolate hardens, about 1 hour. *Makes 30.*

Hanukkah Cookies

Israel

Dough

1 cup butter or margarine, softened
1 package (8 ounces) cream cheese, softened
2 tablespoons sugar
2 cups flour

Filling

½ cup chopped dates
½ cup chopped pistachio nuts
⅓ cup sugar
2 teaspoons cinnamon
¼ cup butter or margarine, softened

Topping

Powdered sugar

To make dough: Beat together 1 cup butter or margarine, cream cheese, and 2 tablespoons sugar in a large bowl until light and fluffy. Add flour and blend well. Shape dough into ball; divide in fourths. Shape each quarter into a ball and flatten into a ½-inch-thick circle. Wrap each circle in plastic wrap; refrigerate 45 minutes or until firm.

To make filling: In a small bowl, combine dates, nuts, ⅓ cup sugar, cinnamon, and ¼ cup butter or margarine. Blend well.

To make cookies: Preheat oven to 375 degrees F. Working with 1 circle of dough at a time, roll dough out on a lightly floured surface into a 12-inch circle. Sprinkle ¼ of date-nut mixture onto circle; press into dough slightly. Cut circle into 16 wedges. Roll up each wedge from curved edge to point. Place on greased baking sheet. Repeat with remaining dough and filling. Bake for 15 to 20 minutes or until light golden brown. Remove from baking sheet and cool on wire rack. Sprinkle with powdered sugar. *Makes 64.*

Tea Cakes

Russia

1 cup butter, softened
½ cup powdered sugar
1 teaspoon vanilla
2¼ cups flour
¼ teaspoon salt
¾ cup finely chopped nuts
Powdered sugar

In a large bowl, beat butter, powdered sugar, and vanilla together until light and fluffy. Add flour, salt, and nuts. Mix well. Roll dough into 1-inch balls and place them on an ungreased baking sheet. Bake at 350 degrees F. for 10 to 12 minutes until set but not brown. While cookies are still warm, roll them in powdered sugar. Cool and roll in powdered sugar again. *Makes 3 dozen.*

Nut Rolls

Hungary

½ cup whipping cream
1 package active dry yeast
¼ cup sugar
½ teaspoon vanilla
3 eggs
3 cups flour
1 teaspoon salt
6 tablespoons shortening
2 pounds walnuts
6 tablespoons honey
½ cup butter
1 cup sugar
1 box (16 ounces) graham crackers
1 box (16 ounces) powdered sugar

Warm cream in a medium saucepan over low heat. Dissolve yeast, ¼ cup sugar, and vanilla in warm cream. Beat eggs and add to yeast mixture. In a large bowl, stir together flour and salt. Cut shortening into flour mixture with a pastry blender until mixture is crumbly. Add yeast mixture and mix into a dough. Knead until smooth. Chill dough for 1 hour in refrigerator.

Grind walnuts and mix with honey, butter, and 1 cup sugar. Crush graham crackers and mix with powdered sugar. Spread half of the crushed graham cracker mixture on a smooth surface. Roll out half of dough on top of crackers to make a rectangle ⅛-inch thick. Spread dough with half of walnut mixture and roll up from long side. Cut in 1-inch rolls. Place on lightly greased baking sheet. Repeat with second half of ingredients. Bake at 400 degrees F. for 18 to 20 minutes. *Makes 3 dozen.*

Jam Cookies *Czech Republic*

1 cup butter, softened
1 cup sugar
2 egg yolks
2 cups flour
1 cup chopped walnuts or pecans
½ cup strawberry preserves

Preheat oven to 325 degrees F. Grease an 8-inch square cake pan; set aside. Cream butter and sugar together in a medium bowl. Add egg yolks and mix well. Add flour gradually, mixing well after each addition. Fold in nuts. Spoon half the batter into the prepared pan, spreading evenly over the bottom. Top with the strawberry preserves. Cover with remaining batter. Bake in preheated oven for 1 hour or until lightly browned. Cut into 1 x 2-inch bars. *Makes 30.*

Date Nut Chews *China*

Crust

¾ cup butter
1½ cups flour
3 tablespoons brown sugar

Topping

2 tablespoons flour
1 teaspoon baking powder
2 eggs, slightly beaten
1 cup chopped dates
1 cup chopped walnuts or pecans
1 cup sweetened, flaked coconut

Frosting

1 cup powdered sugar
Juice of 1 lemon
Cream or soft butter, if needed

Preheat oven to 300 degrees F. Grease a 10-inch square baking pan; set aside.

Make crust: Blend butter, flour, and brown sugar together. Pat the mixture into the prepared pan. Bake in preheated oven for 10 minutes. Remove from oven and reduce oven heat to 275 degrees F.

Add topping: Sift the flour and baking powder together. Add the slightly beaten eggs and stir well. Add dates, nuts, and coconut and mix well. Sprinkle this mixture over the baked crust and bake at 275 degrees F. for 25 minutes.

Add frosting: Combine powdered sugar and lemon juice. If frosting is too stiff, soften it with a small amount of cream or soft butter. Frost bars as soon as they come out of the oven. Cool and cut into squares to serve. *Makes 16.*

Christmas Cookies (Brune Kager) *Denmark*

1 cup butter
1 cup brown sugar
1 cup dark corn syrup
1 tablespoon grated orange peel
1 teaspoon cardamom
1 teaspoon cloves
½ teaspoon salt
½ teaspoon cinnamon
4 to 5 cups flour
¼ cup finely chopped almonds
Split blanched almonds

Melt butter in a large saucepan; add brown sugar and corn syrup. Remove from heat and stir in orange peel, cardamom, cloves, salt, and cinnamon. Add enough flour to make an easily manageable dough. Knead in chopped almonds. Shape dough into two rolls about 15 inches long. Refrigerate dough for up to three weeks. (Dough improves in flavor if it is allowed to remain in refrigerator for this long.) When ready to bake, cut into thin slices and place on lightly greased baking sheet. Decorate each cookie with an almond half. Bake at 375 degrees F. about 8 minutes or until crisp. Cool on wire rack. Store in tightly covered container. *Makes 15 dozen.*

Honey Cakes (Lebkuchen)

Cookies

½ cup honey
½ cup molasses
¾ cup brown sugar
1 egg
1 tablespoon lemon juice
1 teaspoon lemon peel
2¾ cups flour
½ teaspoon baking soda
1 teaspoon cinnamon
1 teaspoon cloves
1 teaspoon allspice
1 teaspoon nutmeg
⅓ cup chopped candied citrus fruits
⅓ cup chopped walnuts, pecans, or almonds

Glaze

1 cup sugar
½ cup water
¼ cup powdered sugar

In a large saucepan, mix honey and molasses together and bring to a boil. Cool thoroughly. When mixture is cool, stir in brown sugar, egg, lemon juice, and lemon peel. Mix well. Sift together flour, baking soda, cinnamon, cloves, allspice, and nutmeg. Add to honey-molasses mixture and mix well. Stir in the candied fruits and nuts. Chill dough overnight.

Preheat oven to 400 degrees F. Roll out a small amount of dough at a time, keeping the rest chilled. Roll dough ¼- to ½-inch thick and cut into rectangles 1½ x 2½ inches. Place 1 inch apart on a greased baking sheet. Bake in preheated oven 10 to 12 minutes or until no imprint remains when cookies are touched lightly.

While cookies bake, make glaze: Boil sugar and water together until mixture reaches a temperature of 230 degrees F. on a candy thermometer. Remove from heat and beat in powdered sugar. As soon as cookies are removed from oven, brush hot glaze thinly over them. (When glaze gets sugary, reheat slightly, adding a little water until clear again.) Quickly remove glazed cookies from the baking sheet and put them on a wire rack to cool. Store 2 to 3 weeks in an airtight container to mellow. *Makes 6 dozen.*

Pictured on page 84

Black-and-White Biscotti

Cookies

3 cups flour
½ cup sugar
½ cup brown sugar
3 teaspoons baking powder
½ teaspoon salt
4 ounces unsweetened chocolate, melted
1 teaspoon grated orange peel
⅓ cup olive oil
¼ cup orange juice
2 teaspoons vanilla
3 eggs
6 ounces white chocolate, chopped

Topping

4 ounces white chocolate, chopped
1 tablespoon shortening

Preheat oven to 350 degrees F. Lightly grease 2 baking sheets; set aside. Stir together flour, sugar, brown sugar, baking powder, and salt in a large bowl. Add melted chocolate, orange peel, oil, orange juice, vanilla, and eggs. Blend well to make a stiff dough. Knead chopped white chocolate into dough. Divide dough into 4 equal parts; shape each part into a log about 14 inches long. Place 2 logs on each baking sheet; flatten with fingers to a width of about 2½ inches each. Bake in preheated oven for 18 to 20 minutes or until firm to the touch.

Remove baking sheets from oven. Reduce oven temperature to 300 degrees F. Cool logs on baking sheets for 10 minutes. Cut warm logs diagonally into ½-inch-wide slices. Place slices, cut side up, on same baking sheets. Bake at 300 degrees F. for 7 to 9 minutes or until top surface is dry. Turn cookies over and bake an additional 7 to 9 minutes. Remove cookies from sheets and cool completely on wire racks.

Topping: Melt white chocolate with shortening in a small saucepan over low heat, stirring until smooth. Drizzle over cookies. Biscotti can be stored in an airtight container for up to 4 weeks. *Makes 7 dozen.*

CAKES

Marzipan Cake *Germany*

2 eggs
3 egg yolks
2 tablespoons milk
½ teaspoon vanilla
¼ cup soft almond paste
1 cup flour
1 teaspoon baking powder
¼ teaspoon salt
1 cup sugar
⅓ cup butter, melted and cooled

Frosting

¼ cup butter
2 cups powdered sugar
1 teaspoon vanilla
Milk

Place a medium bowl in a pan or sink of warm water. Put the eggs and egg yolks in the bowl and let stand.

Preheat the oven to 350 degrees F. Grease a 9-inch square cake pan. Blend milk, vanilla, and almond paste in a small bowl; set aside. Sift flour, baking powder, and salt together; set aside. Remove the bowl with the eggs from the water and beat the eggs with an electric mixer on medium high speed, adding the sugar gradually, until the mixture stands in stiff peaks. Add about ½ cup of this mixture to the almond paste mixture; then return all to the rest of the eggs and blend. Fold in the dry ingredients, ¼ at a time. Blend well. Fold in melted butter. Pour the batter into the prepared pan. Bake in preheated oven for 30 to 35 minutes or until cake begins to shrink from sides of pan and springs back when touched lightly in center.

To make frosting: Beat butter, powdered sugar, and vanilla together, adding milk a teaspoon at a time until mixture reaches desired consistency. Spread over cooled cake. *Serves 9.*

Oatmeal Cake with Caramel Topping *Scotland*

1 cup rolled oats
1½ cups boiling water
½ cup butter or margarine, softened
1 cup sugar
1 cup brown sugar
2 tablespoons light molasses
2 eggs
1½ cups flour
1 teaspoon baking soda
1 teaspoon cinnamon
½ teaspoon salt
¼ teaspoon nutmeg

Caramel topping

6 tablespoons butter or margarine
¾ cup brown sugar
3 tablespoons half-and-half
1 cup sweetened, flaked coconut
1 cup chopped walnuts

Preheat oven to 350 degrees F. Grease and flour a 9-inch square baking pan.

Place oats in a medium bowl and pour boiling water over them. Set aside to cool. In a large bowl, cream butter or margarine; gradually add sugars and blend well. Mix in molasses, eggs, and lukewarm oat mixture. Sift together flour, baking soda, cinnamon, salt, and nutmeg; stir into creamed mixture just until dry ingredients are moistened. Spread evenly in prepared pan and bake for 50 minutes or until cake springs back when touched lightly in center.

To make caramel topping: Combine butter or margarine, brown sugar, and half-and-half in a medium saucepan. Place over medium heat and stir until butter is melted. Stir in coconut and nuts. Bring to a boil, stirring constantly. Boil and stir for 1 minute longer. Spread on hot cake and place under broiler about 6 inches below heat until topping is browned and bubbly. Watch very closely; topping burns easily. Remove from oven and place pan on a wire rack. Let cake cool 30 minutes before cutting. *Serves 12.*

96   Cakes

Pecan Cake

4 eggs, separated
½ cup butter, melted and cooled
½ teaspoon vanilla
⅔ cup sugar
Pinch of salt
⅔ cup ground pecans
⅓ cup flour

Glaze

2 tablespoons butter
½ cup honey

Preheat oven to 350 degrees F. Lightly grease and flour an 8-inch round cake pan. Set aside.

In a small bowl, beat egg yolks, butter, and vanilla. Add ⅓ cup of the sugar and beat until thick and creamy. In a large bowl, beat egg whites with salt until frothy. Continue to beat, adding the remaining ⅓ cup sugar very gradually, until stiff peaks form. Fold ⅓ of the beaten egg whites into the yolk mixture to lighten it. Then gently fold the yolk mixture into the remaining whites until fully blended. Combine nuts and flour and sift one-third at a time over the egg mixture, folding gently after each addition. Any nut pieces too large to sift may be folded in at the end or reground in the blender and sifted in. Pour batter into prepared cake pan. Bake for 30 minutes, or until cake springs back when touched lightly in center. Let cool in pan for 10 minutes; then turn cake out onto a wire rack, right side up, and continue cooling for 1 hour.

To make glaze: Melt butter in a small saucepan over medium heat. Stir in honey and bring to a full boil. Reduce heat and boil gently for 3 minutes. Pour over cooled cake, allowing glaze to drip down the sides. *Serves 6.*

Cream Cake

1½ cups butter, softened
2 cups sugar
3 eggs
1½ cups sour cream
1½ teaspoons vanilla
3 cups sifted flour
2¼ teaspoons baking powder
¾ teaspoon baking soda
⅜ teaspoon salt

Filling

1 cup heavy cream
⅓ cup brown sugar
½ teaspoon vanilla
½ cup chopped walnuts
1 tablespoon sifted brown sugar
Walnut halves

Preheat oven to 350 degrees F. Grease and flour three 9-inch round cake pans.

Cream together butter and sugar in a large bowl. Beat in eggs, 1 at a time; beat until mixture is light and fluffy. Add sour cream and vanilla and beat to blend thoroughly. Sift flour, measure, and sift again with baking powder, baking soda, and salt. Gradually add to creamed mixture. Beat to blend thoroughly. Divide the batter among the 3 cake pans. Bake in preheated oven for 30 to 45 minutes or until cake pulls away from sides of pan and toothpick inserted in center comes out clean. Allow cake layers to cool in pans a few minutes, then turn out onto wire racks to cool completely.

To make filling: Whip cream with ⅓ cup brown sugar and vanilla. Place 1 cooled cake layer on platter; spread top completely to edges with ⅓ of the whipped cream. Sprinkle with half of the chopped nuts. Top with another cake layer, repeat with spreading of cream and nuts. Top with third layer, spread remaining cream over top. Sprinkle with the 1 tablespoon sifted brown sugar and decorate with walnut halves. *Serves 16.*

Lemon Bundt Cake

1 cup margarine
2 cups sugar
3 eggs
2 teaspoons lemon extract
3 cups sifted flour
2 teaspoons baking powder
1 teaspoon salt
1⅔ cups evaporated milk

Preheat oven to 350 degrees F. Grease and flour a Bundt pan.

Cream margarine and sugar together in a large bowl. Add eggs and beat until light and fluffy. Add lemon extract. Sift together flour, baking powder, and salt and add to creamed mixture alternately with evaporated milk, beating after each addition and ending with flour mixture. Pour batter into the prepared Bundt pan and bake for 1 hour. Cool in the pan 15 minutes or less before removing to a rack. *Serves 15.*

Chocolate Cake

Mexico

½ cup margarine
½ cup vegetable oil
1 cup water
2 ounces unsweetened chocolate, or
    4 tablespoons unsweetened cocoa
2 cups flour
2 cups sugar
½ cup sour milk (place 1½ teaspoons of
    vinegar in a cup and fill with milk to the
    ½-cup line to make sour milk)
2 eggs, beaten
1 teaspoon baking soda
1 teaspoon cinnamon
1 teaspoon vanilla

Chocolate icing

½ cup margarine
2 ounces unsweetened chocolate
6 tablespoons milk
3¾ cups powdered sugar (1 pound)
1 teaspoon vanilla
½ cup chopped pecans

Preheat oven to 350 degrees F. Grease and flour a 12 x 8-inch cake pan.

Combine margarine, oil, water, and chocolate in a saucepan and heat until chocolate is melted. In a large bowl, mix together flour, sugar, sour milk, eggs, baking soda, cinnamon, and vanilla. Beat well; then add the margarine mixture. Continue to beat until well blended. Pour the batter into the prepared cake pan. Bake for 35 minutes or until the cake springs back when touched lightly in center.

To make chocolate icing: Five minutes before the cake is done, combine margarine, chocolate, and milk in a saucepan and heat until bubbles form around the edge. Remove from heat and add powdered sugar, vanilla, and pecans. Beat well. (Icing will not be stiff.) Ice cake while it is still warm. *Serves 12.*

Cheesecake with Shortbread Crust *Ukraine*

Crust

1½ cups flour
¼ cup sugar
1 egg yolk, lightly beaten
½ cup butter, softened
1 egg white, lightly beaten

Filling

2 cups cottage cheese
3 large eggs, separated
½ cup sugar
½ cup sour cream
2 teaspoons cornstarch
1 teaspoon grated lemon peel
½ cup chopped walnuts (optional)

To make crust: Stir together flour and sugar. Make a well in the center. Place beaten egg yolk and butter in the well and knead into dry mixture, using your hands, until well blended. Press the dough into the bottom and up the sides of a 9-inch springform pan. Make sure you have a continuous crust all the way around the side of the pan, and make sure the sides meet the bottom crust all the way around. Brush the shell with the egg white, covering both bottom and sides. This will seal dough and keep it from becoming soggy.

To make filling: Preheat oven to 325 degrees F. Press the cottage cheese through a sieve and drain. In a large bowl, beat the egg yolks until light and foamy; then add the sugar slowly, continuing to beat until smooth and light. Add the cottage cheese to the egg mixture, blending well. Stir in the sour cream, cornstarch, lemon peel, and walnuts, if desired. Stir until all ingredients are mixed completely. Beat the egg whites until they form soft peaks; then gently fold them into the batter. Pour the batter into the prepared crust and bake for 1 hour. Cool to room temperature before serving. *Serves 16.*

Birds Milk Cake *Russia*

Cake

½ cup butter
1 cup sugar
2 tablespoons honey
2 eggs
1 teaspoon vanilla
2½ cups flour
1 teaspoon baking soda

Boiled cream

2 tablespoons flour
2 tablespoons sugar
2 cups milk
1 teaspoon vanilla
1 cup butter
1 cup sugar

Gonush

5 tablespoons sugar
5 tablespoons milk
5 teaspoons cocoa
¼ cup butter

To make cake: Preheat oven to 350 degrees F. In a large saucepan, stir together butter, sugar, honey, eggs, and vanilla. Cook on low heat, stirring slowly, until sugar is melted. Remove from stove and add flour and baking soda. Stir until well mixed. Divide dough into 5 equal parts. Prepare five 9-inch rounds of parchment paper by spraying with nonstick cooking spray. Place one of the 5 pieces on each parchment paper and roll out to fit the rounds. Bake about 5 minutes. Let cool.

To make boiled cream: Combine flour, 2 tablespoons sugar, milk, and vanilla in a medium saucepan. Boil, stirring constantly, until ingredients are smooth and thickened. Remove from heat and let cool. Beat butter and 1 cup sugar together until light and fluffy. Add to cooled liquid mixture and beat well. Place 1 layer of cake on platter and spread with cream; top with next layer and continue, spreading cream between each layer. Do not spread cream on top layer.

To make gonush: Combine sugar, milk, and cocoa in a small saucepan; bring to a boil and boil until the mixture is smooth and dark brown in color. Remove from heat and add butter, stirring until butter is melted. Spread on top layer of cake while still hot. *Serves 12.*

Coconut Cake

1 cup shortening
2 cups sugar
4 eggs, separated
½ teaspoon vanilla
½ teaspoon lemon extract
3 cups flour
3 teaspoons baking powder
¼ teaspoon salt
1 cup milk

Coconut cream filling

½ cup sugar
⅓ cup flour
¼ teaspoon salt
2 eggs, beaten
1½ cups milk
¾ teaspoon vanilla
3 tablespoons butter or margarine
½ cup shredded coconut (fresh, frozen, or dried)

Frosting

1⅔ cups sugar
¼ teaspoon cream of tartar
½ cup water
½ cup egg whites
Shredded coconut

Preheat oven to 350 degrees F. Grease and flour three 8-inch round cake pans.

In a large bowl, cream shortening with sugar until light and fluffy. Add egg yolks, vanilla, and lemon extract; beat well. Sift flour with baking powder and salt and add to creamed mixture alternately with milk, mixing well. In a small bowl, beat egg whites until stiff peaks form. Fold into cake batter. Pour into prepared pans. Bake for 25 to 30 minutes. Cool thoroughly.

To make coconut cream filling: Blend sugar with flour and salt in a medium saucepan. Add eggs and milk. Cook, stirring constantly, until mixture thickens. Remove from heat and stir in vanilla, butter or margarine, and coconut. Cool. Put ½ of filling on 1 layer of cooled cake; add the second layer and the rest of the filling. Top with the third layer of cake.

To make frosting: Combine sugar, cream of tartar, and water in a medium saucepan. Cover and heat until mixture boils; remove cover and cook to 260 degrees F. on a candy thermometer. In a small bowl, beat egg whites with electric mixer until stiff peaks form. Pour syrup gradually over beaten egg whites, beating with mixer all the time. Continue beating until fluffy and thick enough to spread. Spread on top and sides of cake. Sprinkle top and sides of cake with coconut. *Serves 12.*

Skillet Cake

⅔ cup flour
1 teaspoon baking powder
½ cup butter or margarine
⅔ cup sugar
2 eggs
2 tablespoons milk

Topping

¼ cup butter
¼ cup sugar
2 tablespoons flour
1 tablespoon cream or evaporated milk
½ cup slivered almonds

Preheat oven to 350 degrees F. Line a 9-inch ovenproof skillet with aluminum foil. Grease and flour the foil.

In a small bowl, sift together the flour and baking powder; set aside. In a medium bowl, cream the butter or margarine and gradually add the sugar. Beat until light and fluffy. Add the eggs, one at a time, and beat for 1 minute after each egg. Blend in half of the dry ingredients; then add milk. Blend well, add the remaining dry ingredients, and blend thoroughly. Pour batter into the foil-lined skillet and bake for 25 to 30 minutes, or until cake springs back without leaving an imprint when touched lightly on top.

To make topping: During the last 10 minutes of the cake's cooking time, combine butter, sugar, flour, and cream or evaporated milk in a small saucepan. Cook over medium heat, stirring constantly, until mixture comes to a boil. Spread over hot cake; sprinkle with almonds. Place under broiler for 1 to 3 minutes or until light brown. *Serves 8.*

Pineapple Nut Cake *Mexico*

1 can (20 ounces) crushed pineapple in juice
2 cups flour
2 cups sugar
2 eggs
2 teaspoons baking soda
1 cup chopped walnuts or pecans

Topping

1 package (8 ounces) cream cheese, softened
2 cups powdered sugar
½ cup butter or margarine
1 teaspoon vanilla

Preheat oven to 350 degrees F. Grease and flour a 13 x 9-inch cake pan.

In a large bowl, combine pineapple with juice, flour, sugar, eggs, baking soda, and nuts. Mix together until well blended. Pour into the prepared cake pan. Bake for 35 to 45 minutes or until golden brown on top. Remove from oven and allow to cool.

To make topping: Blend cream cheese, powdered sugar, butter or margarine, and vanilla in a small bowl. Frost cooled cake. *Serves 15.*

Strawberry-Filled Cake *Finland*

4 eggs
1 cup sugar
1 teaspoon vanilla
¾ cup flour
¼ cup cornstarch
1½ teaspoons baking powder
¼ teaspoon salt

Filling

1 quart strawberries, mashed
1 cup sugar
1 pint whipping cream, whipped and
    sweetened to taste

Preheat oven to 350 degrees F. Grease and flour an 8-inch round springform pan.

Beat eggs until light and fluffy. Add sugar gradually, beating until thick. Add vanilla. Sift flour with cornstarch, baking powder, and salt and fold carefully into egg mixture. Pour into prepared pan and bake for 30 minutes. Cool and remove from pan. Split into three layers.

To make filling: Mix mashed strawberries with sugar. Whip the cream and sweeten to taste. Place the first layer of the cake on a serving plate. Spread ⅓ of strawberries on layer. Spread about ¼ of the whipped cream on top of the berries. Repeat with second layer. Spread the rest of the strawberries on third layer, then frost the whole cake with the rest of the whipped cream. Chill until serving; refrigerate any leftovers. *Serves 12.*

Pudding Cake *Denmark*

1 cup finely chopped dates
1 cup finely chopped nuts
½ teaspoon baking soda
1 cup boiling water
1 cup shortening or butter
2½ cups sugar
4 eggs, beaten
1 teaspoon vanilla
3 cups sifted flour
1 teaspoon salt
1 teaspoon baking powder
1 cup orange juice
Ice cream or whipped cream (optional)

Preheat oven to 325 degrees F. Grease a 10-inch tube pan.

In a medium bowl, combine dates and nuts and sprinkle baking soda over them. Add boiling water, stir, and let set. In a separate bowl, cream together shortening or butter and 1¾ cups of the sugar until fluffy. Add eggs and vanilla and beat well. Sift flour, salt, and baking powder together. Add to creamed mixture. Stir in date mixture. Mix well. Pour into prepared pan and bake for 1 hour and 30 minutes. Remove from pan. Mix remaining ¾ cup sugar with orange juice. Pour over hot cake. Serve with ice cream or whipped cream, if desired. *Serves 12.*

Pavlova (page 115)

Coffee Cake

Germany

4 cups flour
1 cup sugar
4 teaspoons baking powder
¼ teaspoon salt
3 tablespoons shortening
2 eggs
2 cups milk
2 teaspoons vanilla

Topping

4 tablespoons sugar
2 tablespoons flour
2 tablespoons butter, softened
1 teaspoon cinnamon

Preheat oven to 350 degrees F. Grease and flour a 13 x 9-inch cake pan.

In a large bowl, combine flour, sugar, baking powder, and salt. Add shortening and cut into the flour with a pastry blender or fork until well blended. In a small bowl, blend eggs, milk, and vanilla. Combine the milk mixture with the flour mixture and mix well. Pour into the prepared pan and bake for 30 minutes or until a toothpick inserted in center comes out clean. Remove from oven and cool slightly.

To make topping: Mix together sugar, flour, softened butter, and cinnamon in a small bowl. Spread over slightly cooled cake. *Serves 15.*

Banana Nut Cake

Scotland

½ cup shortening
1½ cups sugar
3 eggs
1½ cups flour
1 teaspoon baking powder
⅛ teaspoon salt
4 ripe bananas
1 teaspoon baking soda
¼ cup warm water
¼ cup sour milk, or 1 teaspoon vinegar in
    ¼ cup sweet milk
½ cup chopped walnuts

Preheat oven to 350 degrees F. Grease and flour a 12 x 8-inch baking dish.

In a large bowl, cream shortening and sugar together until light and fluffy. Add eggs and beat well. Sift together flour, baking powder, and salt. Set aside. Mash bananas thoroughly. Add to creamed mixture and mix well. Dissolve baking soda in warm water; add to sour milk and add alternately with flour mixture to creamed mixture. Mix well. Add nuts. Pour into prepared dish. Bake for 50 minutes. *Serves 12.*

Sour Cream Pound Cake

Finland

2 teaspoons butter
1 tablespoon dry bread crumbs
½ cup plus 2 tablespoons butter
1 cup sugar
3 eggs
1¾ cups flour
1 teaspoon baking soda
½ teaspoon cinnamon
1 teaspoon cardamom or ginger
1 cup sour cream
1 teaspoon vanilla

Preheat oven to 350 degrees F. Grease a 9 x 5-inch loaf pan with 2 teaspoons butter. Sprinkle bottom and sides with bread crumbs, tapping out excess crumbs.

Cream butter and sugar together in a large bowl until light and fluffy. Add eggs, 1 at a time, mixing thoroughly after each addition. Sift flour, baking soda, cinnamon, and cardamom or ginger together. Stir ½ of the flour mixture into the creamed mixture. Beat in sour cream and vanilla. Add remaining flour mixture and beat well. Pour into loaf pan; rap pan sharply on table once to remove air pockets. Bake for 50 to 60 minutes or until top of cake is golden brown and springy when touched. *Serves 10.*

Orange Slice Cake

Pakistan

2 cups sugar
1 cup butter
4 eggs
½ cup buttermilk
1 teaspoon baking soda
3½ cups sifted flour
½ pound dates, diced
1 pound candied orange slices, cut in pieces
1½ cups sweetened, flaked coconut
2 cups chopped walnuts or pecans
1 cup orange juice
2 cups powdered sugar

Preheat oven to 350 degrees F. Grease a 10-inch tube pan.

In a large bowl, cream sugar and butter until light and fluffy. Add the eggs, 1 at a time, beating well after each addition. In a small bowl, combine buttermilk and baking soda; add to creamed mixture alternately with 3 cups of the flour. Beat well. Dredge dates, candied orange slices, coconut, and nuts in the remaining ½ cup flour. Add to cake batter and mix well. Pour into pan and bake for 1 to 1½ hours. Meanwhile, mix orange juice with powdered sugar. When you remove cake from oven, pour orange juice mixture over warm cake in pan. Let stand in pan for about 30 minutes. Remove when cool. Refrigerate overnight or longer before serving. The longer this cake sets, the better it gets. *Serves 14.*

Blitzen Cake

Germany

½ cup shortening
½ cup sugar
4 egg yolks, beaten
5 tablespoons milk
1 cup cake flour
1 teaspoon baking powder
½ teaspoon vanilla
4 egg whites
1 cup powdered sugar
½ cup chopped nuts

Filling

Juice of 1 lemon
Grated peel of 1 lemon
1 cup sugar
1 egg, beaten

Preheat oven to 350 degrees F. Lightly grease two 8-inch round cake pans.

Cream shortening and sugar together in a medium bowl. Add beaten egg yolks. Beat until light and fluffy. Stir in the milk. Sift flour with baking powder and add to creamed mixture along with vanilla. Mix well. Pour into the greased pans. Beat egg whites until stiff. Add powdered sugar a little at a time, beating after each addition, until stiff peaks form. Spread on top of batter in pans. Sprinkle with chopped nuts. Bake in preheated oven until browned, about 25 minutes.

To make filling: In a double boiler, combine lemon juice, lemon peel, sugar, and beaten egg. Cook and stir until thick. Let cool.

When cake is done, remove from oven and let cool for 10 minutes. Turn one cake out onto a serving plate, with the nuts and egg whites on the bottom. Spread cooled filling on top of that layer. Place other layer on top of filling, with nuts and egg whites on top. *Serves 12.*

Christmas Cake

1 cup chopped walnuts
½ cup raisins
1 cup mixed candied fruits, such as cherries
    and pineapple (*not* citrus rind)
Flour
1 cup butter
1 cup sugar
4 eggs
1 cup light corn syrup
4 tablespoons granulated molasses (in
    specialty section of supermarket) or dark
    brown sugar
Grated peel of 1 lemon
Grated peel of 1 orange
½ teaspoon cinnamon
½ teaspoon vanilla
4 cups flour
4 teaspoons baking powder
½ cup milk (approximately)

Glaze

Juice of 1 lemon
1 to 2 cups powdered sugar
½ cup ground blanched almonds, or ½
    teaspoon almond extract

Preheat oven to 350 degrees F. Grease and flour three 9 x 5–inch loaf pans.

In a medium bowl, mix together the chopped walnuts, raisins, and candied fruit, dusting with a small amount of flour. Set aside. In a large bowl, cream together butter and sugar. Add eggs 1 at a time, beating well after each egg. Add the corn syrup, granulated molasses or dark brown sugar, lemon peel, orange peel, cinnamon, and vanilla. Beat until creamy. Add 4 cups flour and baking powder. Mix on low speed and add ½ cup milk or enough to make a thick but creamy batter (not runny). Fold in the fruit and nuts. Pour batter into the 3 loaf pans and bake for 45 to 50 minutes or until toothpick inserted in middle of cake comes out clean.

To make glaze: Beat lemon juice with enough powdered sugar to make a glaze that drizzles easily. Stir in almonds or almond extract. Drizzle over warm loaves. *Makes 3 loaves.*

Queen Elizabeth Cake

1 cup dates, chopped or ground
1 teaspoon baking soda
1 cup boiling water
1 cup sugar
¼ cup butter
1 egg, beaten
1 teaspoon vanilla
1½ cups sifted flour
1 teaspoon baking powder
½ teaspoon salt
⅓ to ½ cup walnuts or pecans, chopped or
    ground

Frosting

5 tablespoons brown sugar
5 tablespoons light cream
2 tablespoons butter
Shredded coconut or chopped nuts

Preheat oven to 350 degrees F. Grease and flour a 12 x 8-inch pan.

Place dates in a small bowl. Dissolve baking soda in boiling water and pour over dates. Let stand. In a large bowl, cream together sugar and butter until light and fluffy. Add the egg and beat well. Add vanilla. Sift flour, baking powder, and salt together and add gradually to creamed mixture, beating after each addition. Add date mixture and nuts. Mix well. Pour into prepared pan. Bake for 25 to 30 minutes or until toothpick inserted in center of cake comes out clean. Let cool.

To make frosting: Combine brown sugar, cream, and butter in a small saucepan. Boil for 3 minutes. Spread on cooled cake. Sprinkle with coconut or chopped nuts. *Serves 12.*

Coconut Cream Cake

Italy

½ cup butter or margarine
½ cup shortening
2 cups sugar
5 egg yolks
2 cups flour
1 teaspoon baking soda
1 cup buttermilk
1 cup sweetened, flaked coconut
1 cup chopped nuts
1 teaspoon vanilla
5 egg whites, stiffly beaten

Cream cheese frosting

1 package (8 ounces) cream cheese
¼ cup butter
1 box (1 pound) powdered sugar
1 teaspoon vanilla
1 cup chopped nuts

Preheat oven to 350 degrees F. Grease and flour two 9-inch round cake pans.

In a large bowl, cream together butter and shortening until light and fluffy. Add sugar and egg yolks. Beat well. Sift flour and baking soda together and add alternately with buttermilk to creamed mixture. Continue beating until well mixed. Add coconut, nuts, and vanilla. Mix well. Carefully fold in beaten egg whites. Put into prepared pans and bake for 25 minutes. Cool in pans on wire racks for 10 minutes, then remove from pans to finish cooling.

To make frosting: In a medium bowl, beat together cream cheese, butter, powdered sugar, vanilla, and nuts until very smooth. Spread between layers and on top and sides of cooled cake. *Serves 12.*

Gift Cake

Denmark

2 cups less 2 tablespoons margarine
2½ cups sugar
4 eggs
2½ cups plus 2 tablespoons flour
1 teaspoon baking powder
½ cup warm water
4 teaspoons almond extract
Slivered almonds
Pearl sugar

Preheat oven to 375 degrees F. Grease two 9-inch round cake pans or line pans with waxed paper.

In a large bowl, cream together margarine and sugar until fluffy. Beat in eggs one at a time until light and fluffy. Sift flour with baking powder and add to creamed mixture alternately with water and almond extract. Pour batter into the prepared pans. Sprinkle almond slices and pearl sugar on top. Bake 30 to 35 minutes. *Serves 20.*

Kuchen

Argentina

3 tablespoons butter, melted and cooled
2 egg yolks
½ teaspoon vanilla
2 cups flour
3 teaspoons baking powder
½ cup powdered sugar
Pinch of salt
Pinch of cinnamon
½ cup warm milk (approximately)
⅔ cup jam, any flavor

Preheat oven to 350 degrees F. Grease and flour an 11 x 9-inch jelly-roll pan.

In a medium bowl, blend the butter, egg yolks, and vanilla. In a separate bowl, stir together the flour, baking powder, powdered sugar, salt, and cinnamon. Make a well in the dry ingredients and add the butter and egg mixture; mix until crumbly. Add enough warm milk to form a soft dough. Cover with a cloth to keep from cooling. Take ⅔ of the dough and press into the prepared baking sheet. Top with choice of jam. Roll the other ⅓ of the dough into a thin rope and use the rope to decorate top of cake. Bake 20 to 30 minutes or until lightly browned. *Serves 12.*

Moist Apple Ring

Germany

4 cups peeled, diced apples
2 cups sugar
1 cup walnuts or pecans, broken in
    large pieces
3 cups flour
½ teaspoon cinnamon
½ teaspoon nutmeg
½ teaspoon salt
2 teaspoons baking soda
1 cup vegetable oil
2 eggs, well beaten
1 teaspoon vanilla

Preheat oven to 350 degrees F. Grease and flour a 10-inch tube pan.

In a large bowl, mix apples, sugar, and nuts. Let stand for 1 hour. Sift together flour, cinnamon, nutmeg, salt, and baking soda. Mix oil, eggs, and vanilla together and add to apple mixture alternately with flour mixture. Mix well with a wooden spoon. (Do not use an electric mixer.) Pour into prepared pan and bake for 1 hour and 15 minutes. Remove from oven and let cool for 10 minutes in pans. Turn out on wire rack to finish cooling. *Serves 15.*

Nutmeg Cake

Syria

2 cups brown sugar
2 cups sifted flour
½ cup margarine
½ cup chopped almonds
1 cup sour cream
1 teaspoon baking soda
1 egg
1 teaspoon nutmeg

Preheat oven to 325 degrees F. Grease an 8-inch square baking pan.

In a large bowl, combine brown sugar, flour, and margarine until fine and crumbly. Press ¼ of the mixture into prepared pan. Sprinkle with ¼ cup of the almonds. Mix sour cream and baking soda. Add egg, nutmeg, and sour cream mixture to remaining crumb mixture. Blend well. Pour over almonds. Sprinkle with remaining almonds. Bake for 30 to 40 minutes. *Serves 9.*

Chocolate Oat Cake

Germany

½ cup margarine
1 cup quick-cooking oatmeal
4 ounces sweet cooking chocolate, chopped
1¼ cups boiling water
1½ cups flour
1 cup sugar
1 teaspoon baking soda
½ teaspoon salt
1 cup brown sugar
3 eggs

Topping

6 tablespoons margarine
¾ cup brown sugar
½ cup light cream
½ cup chopped pecans or coconut

Preheat oven to 350 degrees F. Grease and flour a 13 x 9–inch cake pan.

Place margarine, oatmeal, and chocolate in a medium bowl; pour boiling water over them. Let stand 20 minutes. Stir until well combined. In a large bowl, sift together flour, sugar, baking soda, and salt. Stir in brown sugar. Add oatmeal mixture and eggs. Beat at low speed on mixer just until thoroughly combined. Pour into prepared pan and bake for 35 to 40 minutes.

To make topping: Combine margarine, brown sugar, and cream in a medium saucepan. Stir over medium heat until mixture boils; reduce heat and simmer 2 to 3 minutes, stirring frequently, until slightly thickened. Add nuts or coconut. Spread on hot cake and place under broiler 4 to 5 inches from heat until bubbly. (Watch carefully; topping burns easily.) *Serves 12.*

Passion Fruit Cheesecake

Australia

Crust

1½ cups graham cracker crumbs

6 tablespoons melted butter

¼ cup sugar

Filling

2 packages (8 ounces each) cream cheese

½ cup sugar

3 egg yolks

¼ cup flour

1 teaspoon grated lemon peel

2 teaspoons lemon juice

1 teaspoon vanilla

3 egg whites, beaten stiff

½ cup heavy cream, whipped stiff

2 tablespoons passion-fruit pulp, made from
   fresh fruit

To make crust: Blend together crumbs, butter, and sugar. Press mixture into the bottom and partly up the sides of a greased 8-inch springform pan. Smooth the crumb mixture along the bottom to an even thickness. Chill the crust in the freezer for 5 to 10 minutes or until it is set.

To make filling: Preheat oven to 300 degrees F. Beat cream cheese and sugar in a large bowl until light and fluffy. Add the egg yolks, 1 at a time, beating thoroughly after each addition. Beat in the flour, lemon peel, lemon juice, and vanilla until just mixed. Fold in beaten egg whites and whipped cream. Stir in the passion fruit, pour the mixture into the prepared crust, and bake for 45 minutes to 1 hour. Cool to room temperature; then chill. *Serves 14.*

Chocolate Hazelnut Cake

Germany

5 eggs, separated

1½ cups powdered sugar

1 cup ground hazelnuts

1 ounce unsweetened baking chocolate, grated

1 teaspoon lemon juice

½ teaspoon vanilla

2 tablespoons bread crumbs

Frosting

1½ cups powdered sugar

3 tablespoons cocoa

1½ tablespoons melted butter

3 tablespoons warm water

Preheat oven to 350 degrees F. Grease and flour a 9 x 5-inch loaf pan.

Place egg yolks in a medium bowl. Add powdered sugar and beat until creamy and foamy. Add hazelnuts, chocolate, lemon juice, vanilla, and bread crumbs and beat well. Wash beaters thoroughly. Beat egg whites until stiff peaks form. Gently fold beaten egg whites into batter; pour into the prepared pan. Bake for 30 minutes or until toothpick inserted in center of cake comes out clean. Cool cake in pan for about 5 minutes. Run a knife around the inside of the pan and turn cake out of pan onto wire rack to finish cooling.

To make frosting: In a medium bowl, sift powdered sugar and cocoa together. Add butter and stir. Add water a little at a time to make a thick and creamy mixture. Spread over cooled cake. *Serves 9.*

PIES AND DESSERTS

Black Forest Pie
Germany

1 9-inch pastry shell, unbaked

Filling

¾ cup butter or margarine
¾ cup sugar
6 tablespoons unsweetened cocoa
⅔ cup ground blanched almonds
2 tablespoons flour
3 eggs, separated
2 tablespoons water
¼ cup sugar

Topping

⅓ cup sour cream
2 tablespoons sugar
½ teaspoon vanilla
1 cup canned cherry pie filling

Glaze

½ cup semisweet chocolate chips
1½ teaspoons shortening

Preheat oven to 350 degrees F. In a medium saucepan, melt butter or margarine; stir in ¾ cup sugar and cocoa. Remove from heat and allow to cool for 5 minutes. Add almonds and flour and stir well. Add egg yolks one at a time, stirring well after each addition. Stir in water. Beat egg whites at high speed until foamy. Gradually add ¼ cup sugar, beating all the time, until soft peaks form. Fold chocolate mixture into egg whites just until blended. Pour mixture into unbaked pastry shell. Bake for 35 to 45 minutes or until wooden pick inserted in center comes out clean. Cool 5 minutes.

To make topping: In a medium bowl, combine sour cream, sugar, and vanilla. Spread over warm pie. Spoon cherry pie filling over the top and return pie to oven for 5 minutes.

To make glaze: Melt chocolate chips and shortening over low heat in a small saucepan, stirring constantly. Drizzle over pie and refrigerate for at least 2 hours. *Serves 8.*

Kiwi Cream Pie
New Zealand

Crust

1½ cups finely crushed vanilla wafer cookies
   (about 36 cookies)
1 teaspoon cinnamon
⅓ cup melted butter or margarine

Filling

1 envelope (1 tablespoon) unflavored gelatin
½ cup cold water
1 carton (8 ounces) plain yogurt
½ cup sugar
1 tablespoon lemon juice
½ cup whipping cream
2 or 3 kiwi fruits, peeled and sliced
½ cup whipping cream

To make crust: Combine crushed vanilla wafers, cinnamon, and butter or margarine. Press onto bottom and sides of a 9-inch pie tin to form a firm, even crust. Place in refrigerator for 1 hour to chill.

To make filling: Soften gelatin in cold water in a small saucepan. Place over medium heat and cook, stirring constantly, until gelatin is dissolved. Cool. In a medium bowl, beat together yogurt, sugar, and lemon juice; stir in the cooled gelatin mixture. Chill until partially set, stirring occasionally. Beat ½ cup whipping cream until soft peaks form. Gently fold whipped cream into gelatin mixture and chill until mixture holds its shape when scooped into a mound. Spoon into chilled crust. Cover and chill several hours or until set. Just before serving, arrange some of the sliced kiwi around the edge of the pie. Beat ½ cup whipping cream to soft peaks. Spoon into center of pie. Garnish with remaining sliced kiwi. *Serves 8.*

Macadamia Nut Cream Pie

Pacific Islands

Crust

½ cup butter, softened
¼ cup sugar
¼ teaspoon salt
1 egg yolk
½ teaspoon vanilla
1 cup flour

Filling

1 envelope (1 tablespoon) unflavored gelatin
⅓ cup water
3 egg yolks
⅓ cup sugar
1 cup milk
1 cup diced macadamia nuts
½ teaspoon vanilla
1½ cups heavy cream, whipped
Sugar to taste

To make crust: In a large bowl, cream together butter, sugar, and salt until light and fluffy. Beat in egg yolk and vanilla until well blended. Add flour all at once and beat at low speed just until flour is incorporated. Refrigerate dough at least 1 hour. Roll out dough on a lightly floured surface. Line a 12-inch pie tin with the pastry. Prick dough all around with fork. Bake at 325 degrees F. for 20 minutes or until pastry shell is golden brown.

To make filling: In a large saucepan, sprinkle gelatin over water; let stand 5 minutes. Place over low heat and cook, stirring constantly, until gelatin dissolves. Remove from heat and set aside. Beat egg yolks and sugar until thick and creamy. Heat milk in a medium saucepan to just below boiling point; remove from heat. Stir 4 tablespoons hot milk into beaten egg yolk mixture. Return egg yolk mixture to milk in saucepan and cook, stirring constantly, until mixture thickens. Remove from heat, stir in macadamia nuts (reserve some for garnish), vanilla, and gelatin in water, and blend thoroughly. Set aside to cool. When cool, fold in whipped cream, reserving some of the whipped cream for garnish. Pour filling into baked and cooled pastry shell. Refrigerate 30 minutes. Top with additional whipped cream that has been sweetened to taste with sugar, and garnish with diced macadamia nuts. *Serves 10.*

Lemon Curd Tassies

England

Filling

⅔ cup sugar
1 tablespoon cornstarch
2 teaspoons grated fresh lemon peel
½ cup lemon juice
¼ cup water
2 tablespoons butter
3 egg yolks, beaten

Crust

1¼ cups flour
⅓ cup sugar
½ cup cold butter
1 egg yolk, beaten
2 tablespoons cold water

Topping

Fresh raspberries (optional)
Mint leaves (optional)

To make filling: Mix sugar and cornstarch in a saucepan. Stir in lemon peel, lemon juice, water, and butter. Cook over medium heat, stirring constantly, until thickened. Slowly stir about half of the hot mixture into the beaten egg yolks. Then return all of the egg mixture to saucepan and bring to boil again. Cook 2 minutes and remove from heat. Cover with plastic wrap and set aside to cool while making crust.

To make crust: Preheat oven to 375 degrees F. Mix flour and sugar. Cut in butter with a pastry blender until mixture is crumbly. Combine egg yolk with water; add to flour mixture and knead until mixture forms a ball. Divide dough into 24 small balls and press each ball into a mini muffin tin, pressing into bottom and up the sides. Prick with a fork. Bake for 8 to 10 minutes. Cool. Spoon filling into shells. Top each with a fresh raspberry and a mint leaf, if desired. *Makes 2 dozen.*

Apple Pie

Norway

1 egg
¾ cup sugar
1 teaspoon vanilla
¼ teaspoon salt
1 teaspoon baking powder
½ cup flour
½ cup chopped walnuts
1 cup diced apples

Preheat oven to 350 degrees F. Grease an 8-inch pie tin.

Using a wooden spoon, stir together egg, sugar, vanilla, salt, baking powder, and flour. Fold in nuts and apples. Put mixture in the greased pie tin and bake for 30 minutes. Serve warm or cold. *Serves 6.*

Rhubarb Pie

England

Crust

1½ cups flour
½ teaspoon salt
½ cup shortening
1 egg yolk
3 tablespoons water

Filling

2 eggs
1 cup sugar
2 tablespoons flour
½ teaspoon salt
1 tablespoon butter, softened
3½ to 4 cups rhubarb, cut diagonally into
    1-inch pieces

Topping

2 to 3 tablespoons sugar
2 to 3 teaspoons flour
½ teaspoon shortening

To make crust: Preheat oven to 450 degrees F. Sift flour and salt together into a medium bowl. Cut in shortening until mixture is the size of small peas. Blend egg yolk with water and add gradually to dry ingredients, tossing with a fork until well blended. Divide into 2 portions, one twice as large as the other. Set aside smaller portion. Roll large portion out on a floured surface, rolling ¾-inch larger than 8-inch pie tin. Fit pastry into tin. Smooth out wrinkles; flute edges. Bake in preheated oven for 10 minutes. Remove shell from oven and reduce heat to 350 degrees F.

To make filling: Beat eggs until fluffy. Add sugar, flour, and salt. Beat until thick (about 3 minutes). Add butter; stir well. Fold in rhubarb and pour into baked pie crust.

To make topping: Add sugar, flour, and shortening to reserved portion of crust mixture. Mix until crumbly. Sprinkle evenly over rhubarb filling. Bake at 350 degrees F. for 35 to 40 minutes. *Serves 6.*

Flan

Puerto Rico

1 can (14 ounces) sweetened condensed milk
1 can (12 ounces) evaporated milk
4 ounces cream cheese (optional)
3 eggs
1 tablespoon vanilla
1 cup sugar

In a blender, combine condensed milk, evaporated milk, cream cheese if desired, eggs, and vanilla and blend until well mixed. Sprinkle sugar over the bottom of a heavy frying pan. Place over low heat and cook, stirring constantly, until sugar melts and starts to turn golden brown. (Watch carefully; sugar burns easily at this point.) Pour caramelized sugar into an 8-inch round cake pan, tilting pan to coat bottom completely. Carefully pour the mixture from the blender over the sugar. Place the pan in a larger dish or baking pan and fill the larger pan with water to a depth of 1 to 2 inches. Bake at 300 degrees F. for 35 to 50 minutes or until the sides are firm and top is lightly browned. Let cool and flip pan upside down on a plate to serve. *Serves 6.*

Pineapple Cream Pie

Crust

¾ cup butter
1½ cups flour
½ cup chopped nuts

Pineapple filling

1 can (20 ounces) crushed pineapple in juice
⅓ cup cornstarch
4 egg yolks
1 tablespoon water
1 cup sugar
¼ teaspoon salt
2 cups whole milk
2 tablespoons butter or margarine
1 teaspoon vanilla

Cream cheese filling

1 package (8 ounce) cream cheese, softened
½ cup powdered sugar
½ teaspoon vanilla
⅓ cup finely chopped macadamia nuts
⅓ cup reserved pineapple, drained

Topping

1 cup whipping cream
¼ cup powdered sugar
Remaining pineapple, liquid squeezed out
Chopped macadamia nuts

To make crust: Preheat oven to 375 degrees F. In a medium bowl, mix together butter, flour, and nuts. Press into a 13 x 9-inch pan. Bake for 15 minutes or until golden brown. Cool completely.

To make pineapple filling: Measure 1 cup pineapple and juice, reserving remaining pineapple for cream cheese filling and topping (below). Drain juice from measured pineapple. Combine cornstarch, egg yolks, and water in a small bowl. Combine sugar, salt, milk, and drained pineapple in saucepan. Cook over medium heat, stirring constantly, until mixture almost comes to a boil. Reduce heat to low. Add egg yolk mixture slowly, stirring constantly; continue to cook and stir until thickened. Add butter or margarine and vanilla. Remove from heat, cover with waxed paper, and refrigerate 30 minutes, stirring once or twice.

To make cream cheese filling: Combine cream cheese and powdered sugar in a medium bowl. Beat with a fork until blended and smooth. Add vanilla, nuts, and drained pineapple. Mix well. Spread cream cheese filling over cooled crust. Cover with pineapple filling.

To make topping: Whip cream with powdered sugar until soft peaks form. Spread over pie and garnish with pineapple and nuts. (Make sure pineapple is well drained before placing on top of whipped cream.) Serve or refrigerate until ready to serve. *Serves 15.*

Apple Cranberry Dumplings
United States—Amish

2 cups sugar
2 cups water
½ teaspoon cinnamon
½ teaspoon cloves
½ cup butter
2 cups sifted flour
2 tablespoons sugar
1 tablespoon baking powder
1 teaspoon salt
½ cup shortening
¾ cup milk
4 cups grated, peeled apples
1 cup cooked, drained whole cranberries, or
    1 cup whole cranberry sauce
½ cup chopped black walnuts (regular
    walnuts may be substituted)
Whipped cream or vanilla ice cream
    (optional)

In a medium saucepan, combine 2 cups sugar, water, cinnamon, and cloves. Bring to a boil; boil 5 minutes. Remove from heat and stir in butter. Set aside.

In a medium bowl, sift together flour, 2 tablespoons sugar, baking powder, and salt. Cut in the shortening with a pastry blender until mixture is crumbly. Gradually add the milk, tossing the mixture to make a soft dough. Roll dough out on a floured surface to form an 18 x 12-inch rectangle. Spread the apples, cranberries, and nuts over the dough. Roll up like a jelly roll and cut into 1-inch slices. Lay slices in a 13 x 9-inch baking dish. Pour the hot syrup over the slices and bake at 425 degrees F. for 40 minutes. Serve warm with whipped cream or vanilla ice cream, if desired. *Serves 18.*

Treacle Tart

England

Pastry for 2-crust, 8-inch pie
1½ cups light corn syrup
⅓ cup finely chopped almonds
3 slices fresh white bread, broken into crumbs
6 tablespoons heavy cream
1 egg, beaten
Finely grated peel of ½ lemon
Juice of ½ lemon
Milk
Whipped cream or ice cream (optional)

Preheat oven to 375 degrees F. Line an 8-inch pie tin with half of the pastry. Combine corn syrup, almonds, bread crumbs, cream, egg, lemon peel, and lemon juice. Pour into unbaked pastry shell. With second half of pastry, make a lattice for top of pie; brush strips with a little milk. Bake for 35 to 40 minutes or until filling is just set. Serve warm with whipped cream or ice cream, if desired. *Serves 8.*

Holiday Rice Pudding

Denmark

2 envelopes (1 tablespoon each) unflavored gelatin
½ cup sugar
½ cup water
½ teaspoon salt
2 cups milk
1½ cups cold, cooked white rice
2 teaspoons vanilla extract
¼ cup chopped almonds (plus one whole almond)
1 cup chilled whipping cream
Raspberry Sauce (recipe follows)

Heat gelatin, sugar, water, and salt in a saucepan over medium heat, stirring constantly until gelatin is dissolved. Add milk, rice, vanilla, and almonds. Set the saucepan in a bowl of ice water and leave it there for about 15 minutes, stirring mixture occasionally. Mixture should form a slight lump when dropped from a spoon. Whip cream until stiff and fold it into the rice mixture. Pour into an ungreased 1½-quart mold (a ring mold works well). Cover and chill in refrigerator until set (about 3 hours). Turn out onto a serving plate and serve cold with Raspberry Sauce (recipe follows). Note: The Danish tradition is to put one whole almond in the pudding. The person finding the whole almond hides it in his or her cheek. The others try to guess who has found the whole almond. *Serves 8.*

Raspberry Sauce

1 package (10 ounces) frozen raspberries, thawed
½ cup apple or currant jelly
1½ teaspoons cornstarch
1 tablespoon cold water

Bring raspberries (with syrup) and jelly to a boil in a medium saucepan. Mix cornstarch with cold water to make a thin paste; stir into raspberries and bring to a boil again, stirring constantly. Boil and stir for one minute. Serve warm sauce over cold pudding.

Hanukkah Doughnut Balls

Israel

2½ cups flour
1 teaspoon baking powder
2 eggs
1½ cups sour cream
2 tablespoons sugar
1 teaspoon vanilla
¼ teaspoon salt
1¼ cups vegetable oil for deep-frying
1 cup powdered sugar

In a large mixing bowl, combine flour, baking powder, eggs, sour cream, sugar, vanilla, and salt until well blended. (The batter will be soft.) Heat oil in a deep skillet until oil is hot enough to fry a 1-inch cube of bread in 1 minute. Carefully place dough by tablespoonfuls into the oil. Fry doughnuts, a few at a time, for 3 to 5 minutes or until golden brown on all sides. Remove from pan with a slotted spoon. Drain on paper towels. When all doughnuts are cooked, pour powdered sugar into a plastic or paper bag. Add a few doughnuts at a time, close bag, and shake gently until well coated. Serve warm. *Makes 25.*

Butterscotch Apple Tart

France

1 sheet frozen puff pastry, thawed
1 egg white, slightly beaten
2 tablespoons flour
2 tablespoons sugar
2 tablespoons brown sugar
1 teaspoon apple pie spice
1 teaspoon grated lemon peel
2 tablespoons butter or margarine
1 large apple, peeled and thinly sliced
2 tablespoons butterscotch ice cream topping
Whipped cream (optional)

Preheat oven to 400 degrees F. Line a baking sheet with parchment paper.

Roll the pastry out into an 11 x 12-inch rectangle. Cut a 1-inch-wide strip from each 11-inch side; then cut a 1-inch-wide strip from each of the remaining 2 uncut sides. Place pastry rectangle on lined baking sheet; prick with a fork in several places. Brush pastry with beaten egg white. To build up sides, place pastry strips on top of rectangle along edges without overlapping strips (trim where necessary). Brush with egg white. Refrigerate.

Combine flour, sugar, brown sugar, apple pie spice, and lemon peel in a small bowl. Cut in butter or margarine with a pastry blender or fork until mixture is crumbly. Sprinkle half of the mixture over pastry. Arrange apple slices on top, overlapping slightly. Sprinkle with remaining crumb mixture. Bake at 400 degrees F. for 18 to 22 minutes or until pastry is golden brown and apples are tender. Cool 5 minutes. Drizzle warm tart with butterscotch ice cream topping. Serve with whipped cream, if desired. *Serves 8.*

Pictured on page 102

Pavlova

New Zealand

3 egg whites
1½ cups sugar
1½ teaspoons vanilla
1½ teaspoons vinegar or lemon juice
¼ cup boiling water
1 cup whipping cream
½ teaspoon vanilla
Sliced fresh fruit: peaches, strawberries,
     bananas, kiwi, pineapple

Preheat oven to 450 degrees F. Bring egg whites to room temperature. Line a baking sheet with foil. Using an 8-inch round cake pan as a guide, draw a circle on the foil.

In a large electric mixer bowl, beat together egg whites, sugar, 1½ teaspoons vanilla, vinegar or lemon juice, and boiling water. Beat on high speed for about 12 minutes, scraping bowl constantly, until stiff peaks form and mixture holds its shape but is not dry. Spread the mixture onto the circle on the baking tray. Shape into a pie-shell form with a spoon, making the bottom ½ inch thick and the sides 2½ to 3 inches high. Form the edges into peaks or make a rim around the edge. Place baking sheet in center of preheated oven and turn oven off. Let stand 4 to 5 hours. Do not open oven door.

To serve: Remove meringue shell from foil and place on a serving plate. Whip cream with ½ teaspoon vanilla until soft peaks form; spread in shell, reserving ½ cup for garnish. Arrange sliced fruit on top of whipped cream and add the ½ cup reserved whipped cream in the center of the fruit. Cut and serve immediately. *Serves 8 to 10.*

Fruited Doughnut Balls

Netherlands

½ cup milk
2 teaspoons brown sugar
1 teaspoon salt
1 package active dry yeast
¼ cup warm water (110 degrees F.)
1 egg
1½ cups flour
½ teaspoon cinnamon
⅛ teaspoon nutmeg
¾ cup golden raisins
¼ cup chopped candied orange peel
Vegetable oil for deep-frying
Sugar

In a medium saucepan, scald milk; stir in brown sugar and salt and allow to cool to lukewarm. In a large bowl, dissolve yeast in warm water. Stir in the milk mixture, egg, flour, cinnamon, and nutmeg. Beat vigorously with a spoon until batter is elastic in consistency. Stir in raisins and chopped candied orange peel; mix well. Cover and let rise until double (1 to 1½ hours). When doubled, *do not* stir down. Heat oil to 350 degrees F. Dip 2 spoons in oil and drain slightly. Using the spoons, shape dough in 1-inch balls and drop balls immediately into hot oil, cooking a few at a time. Dip spoons in hot oil each time before shaping dough. Fry doughnuts about 3 minutes or until golden, turning once. Drain on paper towels. While doughnuts are still warm, roll them in sugar. *Makes 24.*

Peach Kuchen

Germany

2 cups flour
½ cup sugar
¼ teaspoon baking powder
¼ teaspoon salt
½ cup butter
1 quart peaches, drained, or 7 fresh peaches,
    peeled and halved
¼ cup sugar
1 teaspoon cinnamon
1 cup sour cream
2 egg yolks, beaten

In a medium bowl, sift together flour, ½ cup sugar, baking powder, and salt. Cut in butter with a pastry blender. Press mixture into a greased 13 x 9-inch pan, covering bottom and halfway up sides. Top with drained fruit. Peaches can be halved or sliced. Traditionally they are halved and laid pit side down. Combine ¼ cup sugar and cinnamon. Sprinkle over fruit. Bake at 400 degrees F. for 15 minutes. Blend sour cream and egg yolks. Spread over fruit and bake an additional 20 minutes. Serve hot or cooled. *Serves 12.*

Prune Whip

England

¼ cup sugar
3 tablespoons cornstarch
⅛ teaspoon salt
3 egg yolks
2 cups milk
½ teaspoon vanilla
1 quart small blue prune plums
3 egg whites
3 tablespoons sugar
1 teaspoon vanilla
½ cup chopped walnuts

Mix together ¼ cup sugar, cornstarch, and salt; set aside. Beat egg yolks until lemony in color. In a medium saucepan, scald the milk over low heat. Do not boil. Add the sugar mixture slowly to the scalded milk, stirring constantly until mixture is smooth and starts to thicken. Add beaten egg yolks slowly and continue to cook and stir until mixture has thickened. Stir in ½ teaspoon vanilla. Put plums in a 12-inch glass pie dish and spoon custard over top of plums. (Some of the custard may sink to the bottom.) Whip the egg whites in a small mixer bowl until peaks start to form. Slowly add 3 tablespoons sugar and 1 teaspoon vanilla, continuing to beat until stiff peaks form. Spoon meringue over the top of the custard. Sprinkle chopped nuts over top of meringue and bake in a 425 degree F. oven for about 15 minutes, or until the meringue is golden brown. Remove from oven, let cool at room temperature, and then refrigerate until ready to serve. Spoon into dessert dishes. *Serves 8.*

Marbled Caramel Surprise Pudding *Norway*

2½ cups water
1 cup brown sugar
2 tablespoons butter
1 cup flour
2 teaspoons baking powder
½ teaspoon salt
¼ cup vegetable shortening
1 cup brown sugar
1 cup raisins
1 cup chopped walnuts
½ cup milk
1 teaspoon vanilla
Half-and-half or ice cream

In a medium saucepan, bring water, 1 cup brown sugar, and butter to a boil; boil, stirring occasionally, for 5 minutes. Pour sauce into an 8-inch square baking dish. Preheat oven to 350 degrees F. In a medium mixing bowl, stir together flour, baking powder, and salt. Cut in shortening with a pastry blender. Add 1 cup brown sugar, raisins, walnuts, milk, and vanilla; mix just enough to form a sticky batter. Spoon batter into hot sauce in baking dish by rounded tablespoonfuls. It will spread and sink into sauce as it cooks. Bake in preheated oven for 45 minutes. Serve warm with half-and-half or ice cream. *Serves 6.*

Chocolate Cream *Spain*

4 egg yolks
8 ounces sweet cooking chocolate, coarsely
  chopped
½ cup butter or margarine
4 egg whites
2 tablespoons sugar
Finely chopped orange peel (optional)
Whipped cream (optional)

Beat egg yolks until lemony in color. Set aside. Place chocolate and butter or margarine in a small, heavy saucepan. Heat over low heat, stirring constantly, until melted. Gradually stir about half the chocolate mixture into the beaten egg yolks. Return all to saucepan and continue cooking and stirring over low heat an additional 2 minutes or until very thick and glossy. Remove from heat and let cool to room temperature.

Beat egg whites until soft peaks form. Gradually add sugar, continuing to beat until stiff peaks form. Fold a small amount of the egg whites into chocolate mixture to lighten it; then fold the chocolate into the remaining beaten egg whites. Spoon mixture into dessert glasses by quarter-cupfuls. Cover and place in refrigerator for several hours or overnight. Garnish with chopped orange peel or whipped cream, if desired. *Serves 10.*

Summer Sauce *England*

6 stalks rhubarb, cut into 1-inch pieces
1 cup sugar
¼ cup water
2 pints strawberries, washed, hulled, and
  chilled
8 baked tart shells (optional)
Whipped cream (optional)

Place rhubarb in small saucepan; add sugar and water. Cook over low heat, stirring as little as possible, until just tender. (Add more water if needed.) Cool. Mix in strawberries. Serve in dessert dishes or pour into tart shells and top with whipped cream. *Serves 8.*

Trifle *England*

2 teaspoons cornstarch
2 cups milk
¼ cup sugar
2 eggs, well beaten
½ teaspoon vanilla
1 package (3 ounces) raspberry- or
    strawberry-flavored gelatin
1 package (10 ounces) frozen strawberries,
    thawed, with juice reserved
1 package (10 ounces) frozen raspberries,
    thawed, with juice reserved
1 small angel food cake
2 bananas, sliced
1 cup heavy cream, whipped

Mix cornstarch with a little of the milk in a cup to make a smooth, thin paste. Pour the rest of the milk into a saucepan, add sugar, and heat until almost boiling. Remove pan from heat and stir in cornstarch mixture. Return the the pan to low heat and cook, stirring constantly, until sauce begins to thicken. Remove from heat and stir in beaten eggs and vanilla. Let cool.

Prepare gelatin as directed on package, using berry juices in place of part of the water. Cool slightly. Break cake into small pieces and place half the pieces in the bottom of a trifle dish or large, deep, glass dish. Pour gelatin over cake and let it soak into the cake. Spread half of the custard over the top. Spoon half of the fruit over the custard. Repeat layers: cake, custard, and fruit. Top with whipped cream. *Serves 8.*

Note: Fresh strawberries and raspberries may be substituted, if available.

Raisin Rice Pudding (Rizogalo) *Greece*

4¾ cups *whole* milk
⅔ cup uncooked medium- or short-grain
    white rice
⅓ cup sugar
2 tablespoons butter
1 cinnamon stick
Pinch of salt
⅓ cup golden raisins
2 teaspoons vanilla
2 egg yolks

In a large, heavy saucepan, combine 4 cups of the milk, rice, sugar, butter, cinnamon stick, and salt. Place over medium-low heat, cover, and simmer, stirring frequently, until rice is tender and mixture is creamy (about 1 hour). Remove from heat and discard cinnamon stick. Add raisins and vanilla to mixture and stir.

In a small, heavy saucepan, heat remaining ¾ cup milk just until simmering. Whisk egg yolks in medium bowl to blend. Gradually whisk hot milk into beaten egg yolks. Return mixture to saucepan and cook over medium heat, stirring constantly, until thermometer registers 160 degrees F. (about 2 minutes). Do not boil. Stir egg mixture into rice mixture. Pour pudding into a nonmetal bowl, cover, and chill until cold. Pudding may be prepared a day ahead; keep refrigerated until ready to serve. Thin, if desired, with additional whole milk. *Serves 6.*

Strawberry Dessert *Finland*

5 egg yolks
¾ cup sugar
3 cups crushed (fresh or frozen) strawberries
1 cup cake or cookie crumbs
1 teaspoon almond extract
5 egg whites
Whipped cream

Preheat oven to 350 degrees F. Grease a 13 x 9-inch baking dish and set aside. In a medium bowl, beat egg yolks until light. Add sugar and beat until lemony colored. Stir in strawberries. (If using frozen strawberries, thaw and drain them first.) Mix in crumbs and almond extract. In a separate bowl, beat egg whites until stiff but not dry. Fold into strawberry mixture. Pour mixture into the prepared baking dish and bake for 35 minutes. Serve with whipped cream. *Serves 12.*

Kringle

4 cups flour
3 tablespoons sugar
¾ teaspoon salt
1 cup butter
2 packages active dry yeast
¼ cup lukewarm water
1 cup milk
3 eggs, beaten
1 teaspoon cardamom
Fillings (recipes follow)
1 egg white, slightly beaten
Sugar
Cinnamon
Slivered almonds

In a large bowl, combine flour, sugar, and salt. Cut in butter with a pastry blender. Dissolve yeast in warm water and set aside. Scald the milk, allow to cool slightly, and add gradually to beaten eggs in a large bowl. Add the dissolved yeast, cardamom, and flour mixture. Mix until smooth. Cover and let rise until double (1 to 1½ hours).

Turn dough out onto a floured board and knead gently 2 or 3 times. Divide dough in half and place on 2 large, well-greased baking sheets. Spread dough into a thin rectangle on each sheet. Spread one of the fillings down the middle of each rectangle of dough. Fold 2 long edges in to meet in the center and press together to seal. Brush egg white over tops of loaves; sprinkle with sugar, cinnamon, and slivered almonds. Bake at 350 degrees F. for 30 minutes or until lightly browned. *Serves 20.*

Almond Filling

2 tablespoons butter, softened
¼ cup sugar
1 egg yolk
½ teaspoon rum flavoring
½ cup ground almonds

In a small mixing bowl, beat butter until creamy. Add sugar slowly and beat until fluffy. Beat in egg yolk and rum flavoring. Fold in the almonds.

Raisin Filling

1 cup seedless raisins
1¼ cups water
¼ cup sugar
½ teaspoon grated lemon peel
¼ cup ground almonds

Grind raisins in a food chopper. Place in small saucepan with water, sugar, and lemon peel. Cook over medium heat, stirring constantly, until thick and smooth (about 5 minutes). Cool. Fold in the almonds.

Pears Helène

France

½ cup chocolate syrup
8 small scoops vanilla ice cream
4 canned pear halves, drained
⅓ cup raspberry or strawberry jam
1 tablespoon hot water

If you have them, use glass dessert bowls to show off the layers of this dessert. Put 2 tablespoons of the chocolate syrup in the bottom of each of 4 dessert glasses or bowls. Place 2 scoops of vanilla ice cream on top of the chocolate syrup in each bowl. Place pear half, cut side down, on top of ice cream scoops. Combine jam with hot water and spoon mixture over pears. *Serves 4.*

¼ cup milk
¼ cup butter or margarine
2 tablespoons sugar
¾ teaspoon salt
¼ cup warm water (about 110 degrees F.)
1 package active dry yeast
2 eggs
3½ cups flour
Choice of fillings (recipes follow)
Streusel Topping (recipe follows)
Powdered sugar

In a small saucepan, combine milk, butter or margarine, sugar, and salt. Heat over medium heat just until butter or margarine melts. Let cool to 110 degrees. While milk mixture is cooling, pour water into a large electric mixer bowl. Sprinkle yeast on top of water and let stand until bubbly (about 5 minutes). Pour in milk mixture, eggs, and 2 cups of the flour. Beat on medium speed until batter pulls away from sides of bowl. Add 1 cup more of flour and stir with a wooden spoon to make a soft dough. Place dough on a floured board and knead until smooth and elastic (5 to 10 minutes). Place in a greased bowl, turning once to grease top of dough. Cover and let rise until double (1 to 1½ hours). While dough is rising, prepare filling of your choice and streusel topping.

Punch down dough and turn out onto a greased 14-inch pizza pan or a 10 x 15-inch jelly-roll pan. Invert bowl over the top of the dough and let it rest for 5 to 10 minutes. Then pat dough out to fit pan. Cover evenly with chosen filling. Sprinkle streusel evenly over the filling. Let rise until puffy (about 20 minutes). Bake at 375 degrees F. for 25 minutes or until golden brown. Let cool for 20 minutes, then dust with powdered sugar and serve warm. *Serves 14.*

Apple Filling

5 cups peeled, chopped, tart apples
2 tablespoons lemon juice
1 tablespoon water
¾ cup sugar
2 tablespoons flour
½ teaspoon cinnamon
¼ teaspoon nutmeg

Combine apples, lemon juice, and water in a medium saucepan. Bring to a boil over medium heat. Cover, reduce heat, and simmer, stirring occasionally, until apples are just tender when pierced with a fork (8 to 10 minutes). Combine sugar, flour, cinnamon, and nutmeg in a bowl. Mix well. Stir into apples and cook, stirring constantly, until thickened. Remove from heat and let cool. Spread over crust.

Cream Cheese Filling

1 package (8 ounces) cream cheese, softened
½ cup sugar
1 egg
1 teaspoon finely grated lemon peel
1 teaspoon vanilla
½ cup golden raisins

In a small mixer bowl, beat cream cheese until fluffy. Beat in sugar, egg, lemon peel, and vanilla. Stir in raisins. Spread over crust.

Streusel Topping

1¼ cups flour
½ cup powdered sugar
1 teaspoon baking powder
½ teaspoon cinnamon
½ cup firm butter or margarine,
    cut into small pieces
½ teaspoon vanilla

In a medium bowl, stir together flour, powdered sugar, baking powder, and cinnamon. Cut in butter or margarine with a pastry blender until crumbly. Mix in vanilla. Sprinkle over filling on crust.

Crepes with Strawberries

France

2 eggs
½ cup flour
1 tablespoon sugar
½ cup milk
2 tablespoons water
1½ teaspoons melted butter
3 cups fresh sliced strawberries
⅓ cup sugar
1 cup cottage cheese
1 cup sour cream
½ cup powdered sugar

In a small bowl, beat the eggs; slowly add flour and 1 tablespoon sugar alternately with milk and water. Whisk or beat with an electric mixer until smooth. Beat in melted butter. Put in refrigerator and chill at least 1 hour. Lightly grease a crepe pan or a medium frying pan. Heat the pan over medium heat for several seconds, lift it off the burner, and pour in 2 or 3 tablespoons of batter. Quickly swirl the pan to cover the bottom with a thin, even layer of batter. Set the pan back on the heat and cook the crepe until the bottom is browned. Carefully flip the crepe over with a spatula. Brown the other side, then remove the crepe from the pan with a spatula. Repeat until all batter is used.

Combine strawberries and ⅓ cup sugar in a large bowl. Set aside. Using a blender or electric mixer, blend the cottage cheese until smooth. Add sour cream and powdered sugar and stir well. Put a small amount of fruit down the center of a crepe and top with a spoonful of the creamy mixture. Fold one side of the crepe over the filling and roll it up the rest of the way. Repeat with remaining crepes, using about ⅔ of the strawberries. Top with remaining fruit and sprinkle with additional powdered sugar, if desired. *Makes 6 servings (2 crepes each).*

Jam Pudding

New Zealand

Pudding

1 cup flour
3 tablespoons sugar
1 teaspoon baking soda
Pinch of salt
1 cup milk
3 tablespoons jam (raspberry or strawberry)
3 tablespoons shortening

Sauce

¼ cup sugar
1 tablespoon cornstarch
2 cups plus 3 tablespoons milk
1 teaspoon vanilla

To make pudding: In a medium bowl, combine flour, sugar, baking soda, and salt. Add milk, jam, and shortening and mix until smooth. Pour into a greased 8-inch square or 1½ quart baking dish. Cover with waxed paper, using a rubber band to hold paper in place. Place in a pot of water over medium heat. Cover and boil for 2 hours, adding water as needed.

To make sauce: Mix sugar with cornstarch. Add 3 tablespoons milk and stir until smooth. Combine 2 cups milk and vanilla in a small saucepan over medium heat; stir in cornstarch mixture and bring to a boil. Cook, stirring constantly, until thickened.

To serve: Cut pudding in slices and pour sauce over them. *Serves 6 to 8.*

Carrot Pudding *England*

Pudding

½ cup butter
1 cup sugar
1 egg
1 cup flour
½ teaspoon cloves
½ teaspoon allspice
½ teaspoon cinnamon
½ teaspoon nutmeg
1 teaspoon baking soda
1 cup raw, grated carrots
1 cup raw, grated potatoes
1 cup raisins
½ cup chopped walnuts or pecans
½ cup chopped dates

Sauce

1 cup sugar
1 cup milk
2 tablespoons cornstarch
1 tablespoon butter
1 egg, beaten

Topping

Whipped cream

To make pudding: Cream butter and sugar in a large bowl. Add egg and mix well. Sift flour, cloves, allspice, cinnamon, and nutmeg together and add to creamed mixture. Combine baking soda with carrots and potatoes; stir into batter along with raisins, nuts, and dates. Mix well. Pour into a greased mold or 3-pound shortening can. Place mold in pot of water, cover, and steam on top of stove for 3½ hours.

To make sauce: Sprinkle about ¼ cup of the sugar over the bottom of a heavy skillet. Place over low heat and cook, stirring constantly, until sugar melts and turns golden brown. Add remaining sugar, milk, cornstarch, and butter. Heat until butter melts. Mix a small amount of hot milk mixture into beaten egg and return all to pan. Cook, stirring constantly, over medium heat until sauce thickens.

To serve: Spoon pudding into dessert dishes and pour a small amount of sauce over each serving. Top with whipped cream. *Serves 10.*

Baklava *Greece*

Pastry

1 pound walnuts
1 pound almonds
1 tablespoon cinnamon
1 pound filo dough sheets
1½ to 2 cups melted butter
Whole cloves (optional)

Syrup

4 cups sugar
2 cups water
1 cup honey
1 cinnamon stick
1 slice fresh lemon

To make pastry: Grind walnuts and almonds in a meat grinder or blender. Mix in cinnamon. Set aside. Place filo dough in a bowl and cover bowl with damp cloth, making sure cloth does not touch dough. Butter a 13 x 9–inch baking pan. Place 3 filo sheets on bottom of pan. Spread liberally with melted butter. Sprinkle with some of the ground nuts and cinnamon. Repeat layers, using 2 sheets of filo each time instead of 3, until pan is nearly filled. End with 3 sheets of filo. Cut into diamonds with sharp knife. Place whole clove in the middle of each diamond, if desired. Bake at 300 degrees F. for 55 to 60 minutes. If it gets too brown, cover with foil for the last few minutes of baking time.

To make syrup: In a medium saucepan, combine sugar, water, honey, cinnamon stick, and lemon slice. Boil gently, stirring occasionally, for 10 to 15 minutes. Remove from heat, discard cinnamon stick and lemon slice, and let syrup cool.

Directly after removing baklava from oven, pour half of the cooled syrup evenly over the top. Wait one hour and then pour the remaining syrup over the top. *Serves 18.*

Plum Pudding

England

Pudding

1½ cups chopped, pitted prunes
½ cup orange juice
1 medium apple, peeled and grated
¾ cup chopped walnuts
½ cup mixed candied fruits
1 tablespoon grated orange peel
½ cup butter, softened
1½ cups brown sugar
3 eggs
3 cups flour
1 teaspoon cinnamon
½ teaspoon baking soda
½ teaspoon salt
½ teaspoon ginger
½ teaspoon nutmeg
1¼ cups milk

Sauce

¾ cup butter
1¼ cups powdered sugar
3 tablespoons orange juice
½ teaspoon vanilla

To make pudding: In a medium bowl, soak prunes in orange juice for 1 hour. Stir in grated apple, walnuts, candied fruits, and orange peel. In a large mixer bowl, cream butter; add brown sugar and beat well. Add eggs one at a time and beat until fluffy. Sift together flour, cinnamon, baking soda, salt, ginger, and nutmeg. Add dry ingredients to creamed mixture alternately with milk and mix well. Stir in prune mixture. Grease and flour 1 large or 2 or 3 medium molds or cans. Spoon mixture into containers about ⅔ full. Cover with foil. Place containers on rack in large kettle with 2 inches of water. Steam 2 hours for large or 1½ hours for smaller containers, or until toothpick inserted near center comes out clean. Cool 15 minutes and invert on wire rack.

To make sauce: In a small mixer bowl, beat butter and powdered sugar together until fluffy. Add orange juice and vanilla and beat well.

To serve: Spoon warm pudding into dessert dishes and top with sauce. (Pudding and sauce can be stored in refrigerator up to two weeks. Wrap pudding in plastic wrap and foil. To reheat, return pudding to original mold and steam for 30 to 40 minutes.) *Serves 18.*

Pineapple Kugel

Israel

8 ounces medium-width egg noodles
1 pound cottage cheese
4 eggs
1 can (20 ounces) crushed pineapple, drained
1 cup sour cream
½ cup sugar
½ cup butter, softened
1 teaspoon vanilla

Preheat oven to 350 degrees F. Cook noodles according to directions on package, omitting salt. Drain well. In a large bowl, mix together cooked noodles, cottage cheese, eggs, drained pineapple, sour cream, sugar, butter, and vanilla until well blended. Pour into an ungreased 13 x 9-inch baking dish. Bake in preheated oven for 1 hour. *Serves 12.*

Eve's Pudding   *Canada*

1½ to 2 pounds apples, peeled and sliced
½ cup sugar
¾ cup water

Topping

½ cup butter
½ cup sugar
1 egg
1 cup flour
1 teaspoon baking powder
¼ teaspoon salt
½ cup milk

Custard sauce

¾ cup milk
¼ cup sugar
1 egg, beaten
½ teaspoon vanilla

Preheat oven to 350 degrees F. In a medium saucepan, combine apples, ½ cup sugar, and water. Simmer until apples are tender. Pour into a large deep-dish pie plate.

To make topping: Cream butter and sugar together in a medium bowl. Add egg and beat well. Sift together flour, baking powder, and salt. Add dry ingredients alternately with ½ cup milk to the creamed mixture, beating well after each addition. Spread over top of apples and bake in preheated oven for about 45 minutes or until firm and golden brown.

To make custard sauce: In a small saucepan, heat milk and sugar over medium heat until hot but not boiling. Pour a small amount of hot milk into beaten egg and stir until blended. Pour egg mixture back into the hot milk very slowly, stirring all the time. Continue to cook, stirring constantly, until the mixture coats the back of the spoon. Add vanilla and stir well. Pour hot sauce over pudding. *Serves 10.*

Glazed Nuts   *Sweden*

4 egg whites
2 cups sugar
2 teaspoons salt
1 pound whole almonds
1 pound pecan halves
1 cup butter

In a large mixer bowl, beat the egg whites until soft peaks form. Add the sugar a little at a time and continue beating until stiff peaks form. Add the salt. Carefully stir in nuts until well coated. In a large, shallow baking pan (a broiler pan works well), melt the butter. Spread the nut mixture over the melted butter in the bottom of the pan. Bake at 325 degrees F. for 40 to 50 minutes, stirring every 10 minutes, until nuts are completely coated and start to separate. Make sure to turn the mixture completely over each time to keep it from burning on the bottom. Remove from oven and immediately loosen nuts with spatula to prevent them sticking to bottom of pan. Let the nuts cool completely and place in an airtight container. *Makes 2 pounds.*

Chocolate Balls (Brigadeiros)   *Brazil*

1 can (14 ounces) sweetened condensed milk
¼ cup cocoa
1 tablespoon butter or margarine
6 to 8 tablespoons chocolate-flavored
    sprinkles
Small foil or paper decorator cups

Combine condensed milk, cocoa, and butter or margarine in a medium saucepan. Cook over medium-low heat, stirring constantly, for 7 to 8 minutes or until candy forms a ball around the spoon and pulls away from the sides of the pan. Remove from heat and allow to cool to room temperature. Place chocolate sprinkles in a small dish. Butter your hands and shape cocoa mixture into 1-inch balls. Gently roll balls in the chocolate sprinkles and place in individual decorator cups. Cover and chill before serving. *Makes about 2 dozen balls.*

Pralines

2 cups sugar
1 cup brown sugar
½ cup butter
1 cup evaporated milk
2 tablespoons light corn syrup
4 cups pecan halves

In a heavy pan, combine sugars, butter, evaporated milk, and corn syrup. Heat over medium heat, stirring constantly, until the mixture boils. Reduce heat to low and continue boiling, without stirring, until candy reaches soft-ball stage, 235 degrees F. on a candy thermometer (about 30 minutes). Remove from heat. Beat until mixture becomes creamy and begins to thicken. Add the pecans and drop by teaspoonfuls on wax paper. Cool. Store in an airtight container. *Makes 60 pieces.*

Burnt Sugar Fudge

3 cups sugar
¼ cup boiling water
1 cup milk, light cream, or evaporated milk, scalded
3 tablespoons butter or margarine
¼ teaspoon salt
2 tablespoons grated orange peel
1 cup finely chopped walnuts or pecans

Line a 9 x 5-inch loaf pan or an 8-inch square cake pan with aluminum foil, extending over edges. Butter foil. Set aside.

Sprinkle ½ cup of the sugar evenly over the bottom of a large, heavy saucepan. Place over low heat and cook, stirring constantly, until sugar melts and starts to turn golden in color. (Be careful not to burn the sugar; it burns easily at this point.) Remove pan from heat and carefully stir in the boiling water; stir until sugar is dissolved. Stir in scalded milk or cream and remaining 2½ cups sugar. (Don't worry about the lumps; sugar will dissolve as you cook.) Return pan to heat. Stirring constantly, cook over medium heat until mixture begins to boil. Cook, *without stirring,* to soft-ball stage or 238 degrees F. on a candy thermometer. Remove from heat and drop in butter or margarine and salt. *Do not stir.* Cool mixture in pan until the bottom of the pan feels comfortably warm to the palm of your hand. While syrup cools, place orange peel in a small saucepan and cover with water. Heat to boiling. Remove from heat and let stand a few minutes; then drain and dry peel on paper towel. When syrup is cool, beat with a wooden spoon until it thickens and begins to lose its gloss (about 15 minutes). Beat in chopped nuts and drained orange peel. Spread in the prepared pan and let cool. Cut into squares. *Makes 36 pieces.*

INDEX TO COUNTRIES

INDEX TO RECIPES